For They Shall Be Comforted

For They Shall Be Comforted

GRIEVING THE LOSS OF A CHILD

CAMILLE CALL WHITING

Covenant Communications, Inc.

To my angel babies
Ammon and Kija
and my loving husband,
James

Cover image: In the Arms of His Love © Del Parson. For print information please visit
www.delparson.com.

Cover design copyrighted 2009 by Covenant Communications, Inc.

Published by Covenant Communications, Inc.
American Fork, Utah

Printed in Canada
First Printing: May 2009

16 15 14 13 12 11 10 09   10 9 8 7 6 5 4 3 2 1

ISBN-13 978-1-59811-724-0
ISBN-10 1-59811-724-6

Contents

$\mathcal{P}$reface

MY HUSBAND HAS BEEN TRYING for quite some time to persuade me to write a book on this subject. I resisted, thinking that my experiences would be of no help to anyone else.

A few months after our loss of a second child, I received a phone call from a friend whom I had not seen for a long time. She revealed to me that she had lost twins in a similar manner, and she wanted to talk. As we shared our experiences with each other, I was amazed at how similar they were. Even our feelings and reactions to our situations were alike. At the end of our conversation, we both felt a sense of normalcy that each of us needed. Our circumstances had not changed, but we no longer felt alone.

Babies are born every day. People die every day. But a baby's death does not seem like such a natural occurrence—and definitely not something that would happen to *me*. And yet it did. Because no one plans for this sort of thing to happen, tools are often needed to deal with it when it does. I hope this book will serve as one of those tools.

During the writing of this book, I felt almost naked as I revealed some of my most deeply held emotions and experiences. I realized, however, that this book would be of no value to anyone if I resisted being completely open and honest about my feelings. I hope that the experiences I share in this book will benefit those facing their own grief, as well as those longing to comfort them, and that this book will bring them one step closer to the peace they long for.

Acknowledgments

I WOULD BE REMISS NOT to mention the late Elisabeth Kübler-Ross and her lifelong dedication to the research of grief. Throughout her life she brought comfort to countless individuals as she helped them understand their own feelings of denial, anger, regret, and sadness.

Additionally, I am grateful to those who have shared their own feelings of grief with me over the years and to those who have brought comfort to me during my times of loss. I send a heartfelt thank you to all of the doctors, nurses, and hospital staff who cared for me, Ammon, and Kija.

I wish to thank my editor, Eliza Nevin, for her kindness and perspective in helping me to express my thoughts and feelings in a way that the readers would understand. I'm also grateful to Covenant Communications for recognizing the need for a book of this nature.

To my dear family I express my love and appreciation for their patience as this book came to fruition. I realize that many of the things I share are not only personal for me, but are personal for them as well. I am grateful for their understanding of the need to help others through a similar situation of grief. I appreciate my aunt Patricia Webb for her willingness to allow me to share a portion of her beautiful poem, "Why?" I thank my parents for their example as they dealt with the grief of losing their baby many years ago. Their love and compassion for me helped me greatly years later when I lost two of my own children.

My sweet husband encouraged me to write this book and was completely supportive as I went through the process of writing and editing. I could never put into words my devotion to and love for him. He is my best friend.

And lastly, I am so grateful for my Heavenly Father and Savior Jesus Christ, who were patient with me each time I went through the grief process. I am grateful for the help that I felt from Them as I tried to express my emotions and experiences in a way that would be most helpful to those who are currently suffering from a loss of their own. My knowledge of Their unconditional love for me has been invaluable throughout my life and most importantly during my times of grief.

Introduction

". . . for I do know that whosoever shall put their trust in God shall be supported in their trials, and their troubles, and their afflictions, and shall be lifted up at the last day."

—Alma 36:3

ALL MY LIFE I WAS taught that motherhood is the greatest calling in life, and I never had any reason to doubt it. From my early childhood through my college years, my goals and aspirations were all related to my future motherhood. I planned a life of pure happiness, in which the patter of little feet would be heard throughout the house. While the patter of little feet is not absent from my home, my life has not unfolded completely in the way I had planned.

Cradling my newborn son in my arms as I watched him pass from this life to the next was one of the most beautiful, yet heartbreaking, experiences of my life. Years later, as I held my daughter's tiny lifeless body in my hands, I again felt the reverent yet painful weight of a broken heart. I had naively believed that because my childhood was not void of great sorrow, I should be shielded from life's greatest heartaches as an adult. I believed that I had already experienced my fair share of grief. Deep inside, though, I knew no one had ever promised that life would be fair.

With optimism, I had planned a life of happiness and joy, but somewhere along the way my life's plans had gone off course. Hadn't Heavenly Father known my plans? Hadn't He heard my pleadings to Him to create for me the life, the family, the world of my dreams? How could the life that I had planned have been left by the wayside and replaced with a life full of tragic events and more sorrow than I ever dreamed I would experience? And what heartache was yet in store for me?

These are questions you may be asking as you deal with the loss of a baby and the hopes and dreams you had for him or her and for your life together. Although it is one of the most heart-wrenching trials that a woman can be expected to survive, many of us do experience it. We experience it, we survive it, and we become stronger because of it. While reading this book, you may find similarities to your situation and you may find differences. All of us are unique. All of us will act or feel differently, but there will also be many similarities in our emotions. Understanding and embracing those similarities will help us heal together.

ONE

*C*ory

AT NINE YEARS OLD, I was a typical oldest child, a "little mother" to my younger brothers. My mother was pregnant with my fourth sibling. and I was hoping for, praying for, and dreaming of a little sister. By this time my three brothers were becoming less cooperative when I wanted to dress them up in lacy dresses or have dainty tea parties. I needed a true feminine sibling who was as excited about playing with dolls as I was. My play had become very purposeful now—I was practicing for the new baby. Diapering, dressing, and feeding my dolls would prepare me for the mothering that lay in store. I needed to be ready to help in any way possible.

I remember what my mother was wearing and how she looked on one particular day. I remember feeling excited and full of anticipation as I watched her prepare dinner and she told me she would soon leave for the hospital to deliver the baby. And I remember hoping, as always, for a sister.

I spent that night at my friend's house. We played and enjoyed ourselves, and I felt a greater-than-usual sense of happiness as I waited for the exciting news of the birth of our family's new baby. The next day when my father picked us up from my friend's house, I excitedly raced to the car. I paid no attention to the expression on my father's face, to the words spoken by my friend's mother, or to the quiet drive to our home. My friend later told me that she could tell by the look on my dad's face that something was wrong. I didn't notice any of this. I assumed that his prolonging my suspense could mean only one thing—I finally had a sister!

Upon our arrival home, my dad sat my brothers and me down on the couch in our basement to tell us about our new sibling. At first he told us that we had another brother, and I moaned in disdain. Then he went on to further explain that this baby boy, named Cory, was not alive when he was born. "Stillborn" was a term I had never heard, and in my nine-year-old mind, it sounded foreign and cold.

I started asking questions. How could this happen? What was wrong with him? Why couldn't the doctors save him? My dad patiently answered my questions, but the answers did not change the reality that my baby brother was not coming home from the hospital.

Not wanting to hear any more, I ran to my bedroom and fell onto my bed sobbing. My dad soon followed, sat beside me, and wrapped his arms around me while I cried. One of my younger brothers entered my room and watched me curiously, not fully understanding what had happened. I was his protector, and I knew that I should not allow him to see me in such a state of weakness, but I couldn't help it. I had never felt such sadness in all my young life. I cried until I was sure there were no tears left.

My mother returned from the hospital soon thereafter. I don't remember a lot about my activities during the first few days after my brother's delivery, but I do remember standing outside my mother's bedroom door listening to her quiet crying. One time my father opened the bedroom door quickly to go inside, and I caught a glimpse of my mother in her bed, clutching a blanket my grandmother had lovingly stitched for Cory. My heart ached for her. I wanted so desperately to make all of her hurt go away. I wanted *my* hurt to go away.

A few days later at my brother Cory's viewing, I saw the sad faces of my extended family, the tears of my mother, the sober face of my father, and the supportive friends who came to offer their condolences. I remember bouncing up and down on the chairs in the Relief Society room, trying very consciously to appear happy—trying to hide my broken heart as best I could.

Before they closed Cory's casket, my mother leaned over and gave him a kiss. She asked if I would like to see him one last time before the casket was closed. I remember peering over the edge of the casket and looking for the last time at my baby brother's body with the reverence that I knew he deserved, yet self-consciously realizing that people were watching me. I thought perhaps they expected me to burst into tears and run out of the room, but I decided that I was too strong to do something like that. I would prove to the world that I was invincible, that nothing could hurt me. Deep inside, however, I was awakening to the realities of life. I was certain no child should ever have to endure such heartache. And aside from the intense sadness I felt, I also felt very guilty. I knew that somehow all of this was my fault. Perhaps I had wished too wholeheartedly for a sister. Perhaps the cross words I spoke to my family members had somehow caused my brother to die. Perhaps I just wasn't a good enough person to have a healthy baby brother this time.

A couple of days after my baby brother's funeral, I suddenly brightened with a wonderful idea. I ran upstairs to the fridge and pulled out an orange. I began gathering small blankets. My dad saw my activity and excitement and asked what I was doing. I was just about to draw a face on my orange, and I explained that since Mom didn't have a baby, I was going to make her a pretend one to cheer her up. My dad gently told me that this would only make my mom feel sadder, that it would remind her of the real baby that she didn't have. I was disappointed, frustrated, and out of ideas. I wished I could wipe away my mother's pain and bring her only happiness for the rest of her life. I felt powerless and small in this big, mean world.

Over the many years that followed, my mother delivered one more healthy baby: my brother Casey, a miracle baby born amidst several miscarriages and a battle with endometriosis that finally ended with surgery that would abolish all of my mother's hopes of having any more children after Casey. The sister I dreamed of never came.

My childhood experience with sorrow provided me a window into "real life." I watched my parents grieve. I watched the way other people reacted to my parents' grief. I remember overhearing a lady tell my mother, "If you ever want to hold a baby, you can always come hold mine." Even in my nine-year-old mind and heart I realized the inadvertent cruelty of this statement; it was as if she were mocking my mother because she had a healthy, living baby while my mother did not.

I also saw many people treat my family with great kindness. Meals were brought in, and people helped around the house. My aunt brought me and my brothers a bucket full of surprises to open each day during those first couple of weeks without our baby brother.

Although Cory did not live outside the womb, my family believes that he had a spirit because of spiritual experiences we have had. My brothers and I feel that he continues to watch over us. When we were growing up, each year our family made a promise to him of something we would work on throughout the year to better ourselves. We all wanted to live in such a way that we would be worthy to be with him for eternity. This positive memorial to Cory helped me to realize that the death of a loved one could yield positive results.

I know that many things happened behind closed doors, but my parents did not actively try to shield me from their own feelings of grief. Neither did they try to prevent me from expressing mine. While it hurt me to see my parents hurting, it was one of the greatest gifts they could have given me. Years later, I was grateful to have been taught by example how to lovingly grieve with my children—a lesson that I hoped I would never need, but did.

TWO

*A*mmon

JAMES AND I MET IN a social problems class at BYU. As we dated, we soon realized we had both found the eternal companion we had been looking for. We shared the same values, including family, education, hard work, and a love of the gospel. We both wanted to have a large family. We were married in the Bountiful Temple on the day it opened for operation.

Less than a year after we were married, James and I welcomed our beautiful son Cameron into our family. Eleven months later, our second son, Micah, joined us. Less than three years into our marriage and after experiencing my first two pregnancies void of problems, I entered my third pregnancy with optimism. My plans for a house full of children seemed to be coming to pass as I had hoped. Being a mother was everything I had dreamed of and more. My energetic little boys brought me immeasurable happiness, and I couldn't wait to add another child to the crew. My doctor visits gave me no reason to worry about my baby's well-being. I would later realize that subconsciously I'd had a feeling all along that something would go wrong, but for the most part I felt very happy and at ease.

I loved being pregnant. I rarely had morning sickness. Although I gained more weight than I would have liked, having a healthy baby was more important to me than how I looked. I tried to enjoy every minute of each of my pregnancies because I knew that I would never again be that physically close to my precious little ones.

During my thirty-third week of my third pregnancy, I went to the hospital for a very extensive ultrasound. Because the ultrasound technician did not have another appointment after mine, he was very thorough, with the ultrasound lasting more than an hour. All appeared to be well. My baby was positioned head down, ready to deliver. When I met with my doctor afterward he had no concerns. After I mentioned having quite a few Braxton-Hicks contractions, my doctor advised me that if I had more than four in an hour, I should call him.

My husband was employed by the Boy Scouts of America as a district executive at that time. Within a week of my ultrasound, James went out of town for a weeklong training camp near Denver, Colorado—about six hours from our home in Moab. One of my college roommates was getting married in the Denver Temple the following weekend, so we made plans to meet up in Denver and follow each other home. Soon after James left, however, the Division of Child and Family Services (DCFS) called and asked me to take a foster child. We'd been foster parents for a few years, and it seemed that the calls to take a child never came at a convenient time. However, I could never bear to tell them no. A caseworker brought me a toddler with a broken leg, giving me no timeline for the length of his stay. I decided that if our foster son was still in our home when it was time to leave for the wedding, I would not go.

I realized that in addition to this obstacle, the expiration date of my temple recommend had sneaked up on me. Fortunately, my very dedicated bishop arranged to leave his other duties to come to the church and interview me. I was also able to arrange an interview with a member of the stake presidency on short notice—nothing short of a miracle.

A few nights later I started having multiple Braxton-Hicks contractions. Though painless, I worried about what my doctor had told me. I called him at the hospital, where he was in the process of delivering babies for two or three women, and asked if I ought to come in. He thought about it and then reluctantly told me no, probably because of his high caseload that night. I have often wondered what might have happened if I'd decided to go into the hospital instead of calling first. But just as quickly, I've dismissed the thought, realizing that I can't change anything about the way things have come to pass.

Two days before I was scheduled to leave for Denver, I had almost completely given up on going because the foster child was still in my care and I didn't want to force DCFS to move him just so I could go on vacation. That afternoon our foster son went to a home visit and never returned. I started pacing the floor. Finally at about 9:00 PM I called his caseworker at home. "Oh, I forgot to call you!" he said. "We've decided to return him home. The allegations were unfounded. I'm sorry I didn't let you know." Suddenly I had no reason to cancel my trip to Denver.

Whenever doubts creep into my mind about how the events of the next few days occurred, I often remember the days preceding my trip and realize that angels must have been orchestrating the details because it all seemed to come together so well. If things had not fallen into place for my trip, Ammon would probably have been stillborn in our small town with no medical equipment capable of reviving him while my husband was several hours away.

Early in the morning I loaded Cameron, two-and-a-half years old, and Micah, one-and-a-half years, into our small car and started on our six-hour trip to Denver. I distinctly remember feeling hiccups from the baby as I was driving out of town. I smiled to myself because I loved every reminder I felt from my little companion. That was the last time I remember feeling him move.

Just as we were nearing Denver, we encountered a rainstorm such as I had never before experienced. It was as if sheets of water were pouring on us. My windshield wipers could not keep up. Because I was not used to all the traffic on the interstate, I became very nervous. I took a wrong turn, which delayed my arrival and made me even more anxious. Finally I reached the house of an acquaintance who had arranged a babysitter for Cameron and Micah, and he gave me directions to the temple.

Within an hour I was seated in a sealing room in the Denver Temple, feeling very relieved and at peace. My friend's ceremony was beautiful, and after the ceremony we went outside to take pictures. As we were standing together for one large group picture, I experienced a major contraction—the first painful one I'd had during the pregnancy. I didn't worry, however, for my baby's welfare. Contractions had become part of my life at that point, and I dismissed this one as simply a result of the stress of the day.

I enjoyed the wedding dinner after leaving the temple. After I picked up my boys from their babysitter, my friend directed me to a hotel where I was able to find a room on short notice. I called James to let him know where I was, and we made plans to meet the next day. The boys and I relaxed for a while, then I put them to sleep in the cribs that the hotel had provided.

It was not until after they were sound asleep that I realized I hadn't noticed the baby move since his hiccups that morning. Knowing I tended to overreact about little things, I decided to remedy the problem by taking a bath. Usually baths would liven him and he would move around and kick. My concern began to deepen, however, when the bath didn't help. I decided to go down the hall to the candy machines and buy a candy bar. I was sure the sugar would wake him and I'd realize that I had been worrying needlessly. I ate the candy bar quickly, lay down on my side with my hands on my stomach, and waited for him to kick. Nothing.

I wondered if I ought to call the hospital but decided to call James instead. By now it was past midnight, and I had obviously awakened one of the camp leaders. I asked if James was there with him, and he explained that James was in a tent somewhere amidst a great number of other tents and he would have to search each tent in order to find and wake him. He asked if I'd like him to do that and I declined, saying that I didn't think it was an emergency and not to wake him. I apologized for the trouble and hung up.

Still feeling nervous, I pulled out the phone book and looked up a hospital. I found a Seventh-day Adventist hospital and called their labor and delivery department. They told me that I'd better come in and be checked just to be sure and gave me directions to the hospital. So at 1:00 AM I picked up Cameron and Micah and carried them past the front desk and a confused attendant into the pouring rain to find our car in the parking lot. Not knowing where I was or which direction I was going, I started heading down a road. I thought I was following the directions given to me by the nurse at the hospital, but after about fifteen minutes I realized I was going the wrong way. I turned the car around and eventually found the hospital. I didn't know it at the time, but that wrong turn that delayed me half an hour may have provided just the right timing Ammon needed to live the two days he did. A nurse was waiting for me at the door with a wheelchair. I laughed and said, "I'm not in labor. Everything is probably fine." She assured me that it was hospital policy and asked for the help of another nurse to push my boys in their stroller.

The nurses were all very kind. They told me they would not check me in officially but would just put a monitor on my belly and make sure the baby was all right. Cameron and Micah were now wide awake and climbing all over the furniture and me. The monitor was put in place. The second I heard my baby's heartbeat I breathed a sigh of relief and then felt very silly and embarrassed for causing any kind of alarm or imposition on the hospital staff. The monitor had been on for twenty minutes when the nurse told me all appeared to be well. The boys continued to climb over and around me on the bed.

Suddenly my baby's heartbeat went down to 109, and then down to 90. The nurse assured me that the heart rate should go right back up momentarily. It didn't. She called for someone to come take the boys, and she wheeled in an ultrasound machine. She told me that because his heart rate had dropped, I would probably have to stay and be monitored all night. I realized that if I hadn't taken that wrong turn delaying my arrival at the hospital, my baby's dropping heart rate may not have been caught. I would have been sent back to my hotel, and my baby probably would have died inside me during the night.

The doctor came in then, looked at my baby on the monitor, and said, "I'm getting a 60 heart rate, now a 40. We need to deliver now."

I stammered, "But if the baby is born now, won't he have to be in ICU?"

He repeated, "We need to deliver now. If we don't, your baby will die."

The nurses, who, I sensed, had received a reprimand for not checking me in earlier, quickly took my information and filled out paperwork. They told me to contact my husband, so while the nurses were pulling off my clothes to put a hospital gown on me, I was dialing the Scout camp. I again reached the camp leader and told him that this time it really was an emergency, and that I needed James to call the hospital immediately. After being stripped completely naked and draped in a hospital gown, I was wheeled into the operating room on the bed. A nurse assured me that she would watch my boys during the C-section.

While I realized that everyone around me was hurrying as quickly as they could to prepare me for surgery, it felt like the moments were going by in slow motion, as if I were in a dream. I remembered my two vaginal deliveries, which were so incredible and blessed with the feeling that heaven was near. Heaven felt very far away now. I was in a large city where I knew only a few people. I felt completely lost and alone. I lay on the operating table with two bright, round lights above my head. They looked like UFOs. My gown had been pulled up to my chin, and as I lay there completely naked, I started shaking uncontrollably. I asked the nurses, trying to sound lighthearted, "Am I shaking because I'm cold or because I'm scared?" One of the nurses said, "Probably both." I looked around at all of them with their blue caps and masks on with only their eyes visible and asked, "Are any of you LDS?" I was hoping that amidst the preparations for my surgery I might be able to receive a quick priesthood blessing. "No," they all shook their heads.

The doctor entered the room, obviously ready to begin, and a nurse leaned over the top of my head and said, "God will be with you." She placed a mask over my mouth and nose, and I was suddenly asleep. I don't know what I dreamed while I was asleep, or if I dreamed at all. The next thing I remember was a nurse saying, "Camille, can you open your eyes?" and another nurse kneading my stomach. I started screaming in pain, begging for an epidural. "You're hurting me!" I cried. The nurses assured me that they had to knead my stomach to get my uterus to contract. I was aware that my husband was there, although I don't remember anything he said to me. He told me later that when he arrived, I was screaming, "Where's my baby?" Then the doctor pulled him aside and said, "You're going to have to make some tough decisions about your baby." I don't remember any of this.

I also wasn't aware of James's traumatic journey to the hospital. The camp leader had gone from tent to tent until he found James, told him to call the hospital, and gave him the phone number. James gathered his things and made the phone call. The nurses would not give him any information, but just told him to come directly to labor and delivery and gave him directions. I still have the crinkled paper with his scribbled directions on it. Thinking the worst, James sped to the hospital. He was at least sixty miles away at a remote Boy Scout camp, but he made it to the hospital at the same time I was waking up from surgery. He told me that he ran through a toll road without paying because he simply didn't have the time to find some change. Upon arriving at the hospital, he was taken to see the baby first, then our boys, and finally me. His experience was at least as traumatic as mine. Later he told me that he felt like a little boy being thrown into a grown-up world with truly heart-wrenching decisions to make.

After I was cleaned up from the surgery, the nurses moved me to a wheelchair and pushed me into the NICU to see my baby. I didn't know the gender during the pregnancy, and I don't remember who told me it was a boy. I suppose that after having two boys already, it wasn't a huge surprise that I'd had another one. We had already picked out the name Ammon for a boy, so we told the nurses and they scurried to put a label on his isolette. I remember being wheeled up next to his isolette and seeing all the tubes attached to him, including a tube in his mouth that was controlling his breathing. I reached out and touched him, being assured by the nurses that my touch wouldn't hurt him. He did not react. He lay very still with his eyes closed. On the outside Ammon looked perfect; nothing was missing. He wasn't even really that small. He just looked like a normal, perfect baby. That is what I tried to convince myself that he was, despite what any of the doctors or nurses told me to the contrary.

A nurse came to visit me and told me word had spread that I was LDS. She told me she was also LDS and asked if I'd like to have her husband come assist my husband in giving me and my baby a priesthood blessing. I gratefully agreed, and her husband soon arrived. Because I was not yet able to move around on my own, he and James went to the NICU by themselves to give Ammon his blessing. When they came to my room afterward, he told me that my husband had given a beautiful blessing and that he was confident Ammon would be fine. I clung to those words, deciding they would bear much more weight than any medical diagnosis.

After my C-section I was prescribed a number of drugs to help lessen my pain, but these drugs made me very sleepy. The recent delivery also made me feel very hot and sweaty. In order to keep the babies comfortable, the NICU was kept at a very high temperature. I didn't want to leave Ammon's side, but I could stand to be in the NICU for only short periods of time before I became tired, uncomfortable, and sweaty. In desperation I would return to my room, where the air conditioner was on full blast, and quickly fall asleep. I felt guilty that I wasn't with my son at all times. I expected myself to be strong enough to be able to overcome my body's physical weaknesses despite the trauma caused by my C-section and the side effects of the painkillers that I was taking. Each time I returned to my room I felt defeated and guilty that I was not physically able to care for my baby—even if caring for him meant only sitting next to his isolette and watching his little chest move up and down.

The doctor who had performed my emergency C-section came to visit my husband and me in my room. I wanted an explanation. How could my baby's heart rate have gone from totally normal down to 40 so quickly, and what had caused his vegetative state? He explained that Ammon's umbilical cord had had two knots in it about five inches apart, and they'd been depriving him of oxygen for an unknown amount of time. He told me that the chances of that happening were 1 in 10,000. Ammon was also lying breach in the womb, which meant that some time after my ultrasound a week earlier, he had turned completely upside down without my noticing. He was not breathing when he was born, but the medical team was able to revive him after approximately ten minutes. He told me that as far as my health was concerned, I was fine. I would recover fully and would be able to have more children. I could even deliver vaginally again. My health would return to normal within several weeks. He offered no such hope for my baby.

During that first day in the hospital, I was aware of many tests being performed on Ammon. The doctors and nurses carefully and compassionately explained the results of these tests. I chose to ignore their grim diagnoses, clinging to my interpretation of Ammon's priesthood blessing—he would be fine. *He would be fine!*

My parents soon arrived in Denver, an eight-hour drive for them. After visiting Ammon and me, they took Cameron and Micah and went to stay with distant relatives, coming to the hospital often to visit us. My husband went to the hotel to check out of my room. He was refused entrance to the room because I was the one who had paid for it. When he explained that I'd had a baby during the night, they promptly unlocked the door so he could gather my things. As he was leaving, they happily gave him a gift basket and said, "Congratulations!" I am sure he took the basket gratefully without sharing any of the details. In most cases, the birth of a baby would be reason for congratulations. Usually a new father would be joyfully spreading his happy news, not contemplating the painful decisions that lay ahead.

Going back and forth from my room to the NICU, I often met the glances of the many nurses and doctors who were caring for Ammon. The sympathy in their eyes told me what I already knew. My baby wasn't fine. He still had not opened his eyes, and although he had many mini-seizures, he never moved his body voluntarily. He lay perfectly still and quiet, never whimpering, never responding in any way to the world around him. No one ever used the word *coma* to describe his condition, but that is how he appeared to me. As I watched the nurses gently care for him, I knew they were hoping that I would come to terms with his condition. Still, I continued to hope he would just suddenly open his eyes and let out a cry. Miracles had happened to other people before; wasn't my baby deserving of a miracle too? Over and over I silently pleaded with Heavenly Father to heal my son. I believed that He could heal Ammon if He wanted to, but I suddenly doubted my own worthiness. Was this a punishment for something I had done? Was I the one not deserving of a miracle?

Patiently, the doctors continued to give me the same diagnosis: Ammon would not recover. I continued to resist them, feeling that if I lost hope I would be giving up on my baby. I just couldn't do that. He needed me to believe in him, to believe that he could recover and lead a normal life. If his own mother didn't believe in him, who would?

The next day a pediatric specialist came to meet with us in my room. We'd become accustomed to the compassionate and sensitive treatment of the other doctors and nurses, but her demeanor was very different. I sensed that she had become impatient with my denial of Ammon's condition. In what I felt was a cold manner, she explained that all of Ammon's organs had shut down, that his heart was continuing to beat only because of a machine, and that he had no hope for a normal life. His heart could be kept beating indefinitely, but he would never open his eyes, never eat on his own, never react or be a part of our family's activities. He would, basically, be a vegetable his entire life. I just looked at her, wondering how anyone could be so coldhearted—though she may have just been telling us the reality we needed to face. She wanted permission to remove Ammon's life support. I told her we would have to think about it. Obviously perturbed, she left the room.

James and I looked at each other, not sure what to say. We both knew that what she had told us was true. We knew that prolonging our decision was not going to change its outcome. We had to prepare ourselves to say good-bye.

A hospital employee entered my room and told us he was filling out forms for our baby's social security number. We looked at each other and then explained to him that our baby wasn't "viable," as the doctors had put it. Why would he need a social security number? Obviously embarrassed, he apologized and told us he hadn't known about our situation. He quickly handed us the paperwork and exited the room. Soon thereafter the nurses posted a sign on my door telling visitors to check in with the nurses' station before entering. Uninvited visitors were no longer entering my room, but the sounds of babies could still be heard ringing throughout the department. I had been placed in a corner room where the nurses hoped I would be shielded from such noises, but I still heard them. I still saw the babies when I walked past the nursery, and I still knew they were there. Healthy babies and happy parents totally unaware of our worry and heartache.

At the request of James's mother, a counselor from LDS Social Services came to visit me. He was concerned that I had the drapes closed. I explained that the sky was too cloudy outside and I didn't want to see it. It reflected too closely my own feelings of hopelessness. We talked for a while and he left with an offer to call him at any time.

My parents were each able to hold and rock Ammon with his tubes dangling over the edge of his blanket. Cameron and

Micah were brought in to see him, although they both seemed afraid of him, and neither wanted to touch him. He probably looked like a silent alien to them with all of his tubes poking out in every direction. My mom was grateful for the time she was able to spend with Ammon while he was alive because she had never had that time with Cory. She and I both noticed that Ammon's facial features resembled Cory's. The thought of Cory being there to greet Ammon in heaven brought both of us comfort.

After being informed of Ammon's latest test results the next morning and seeing that there was no change, James and I decided that we would take Ammon off life support. My mom went shopping for a white suit, and although she couldn't find one small enough, she brought one to us that we assured her would be fine. She also bought Ammon a beautiful white blanket. James gave Ammon a name and a blessing, and we asked my parents to visit him one last time, then take our boys and go back home. We wanted to be alone for Ammon's death. My mother resisted slightly, saying that I would need her after he died, but we insisted, and they respected our wishes.

We were able to take family pictures with Ammon while he was still alive. Then we said good-bye to my parents and our two sons and they left.

That afternoon James went to run some errands for me and I went into the NICU to hold Ammon. I held and rocked him, tears rolling down my cheeks. This was the first time I had allowed myself to really cry. Some tears had been shed over the past two days, but I had always stopped myself, feeling that I needed to be strong. I was trying so hard not to give up on my little boy, and I thought crying would only reveal my own doubts as to his outcome. Now I let those tears flow.

One of the nurses happened to see me and rushed to get a box of tissues. She pulled the curtain around me for privacy from the other mothers, babies, and nurses. I just sat there and held him, rocked him, and cried. Later I wrote in my journal:

We knew Ammon would be on life support and in the same unconscious state he was in forever and there was no hope of a recovery, so we knew that we needed to discontinue life support and leave him in Heavenly Father's hands. The question was when. James wanted to do it right away (Saturday day). I wanted to wait until Sunday day. We compromised and chose Saturday night. I would have been more stubborn about keeping him longer, but as I held him on Saturday afternoon he seemed to me to be suffering. The nurses all assured us that he was not suffering or in any pain at all. But I felt like he was suffering—maybe not physically, but at least in spirit.

While I held him, I suddenly knew that my baby needed me to let go.

That evening James and I gave Ammon a bath. James gave him one last blessing, this time releasing him from this life and giving him the choice of when he left. I dressed him in his little white suit. The nurse attached his breathing tube to an oxygen tank and followed us into my room. She told us that he might try to breathe on his own for as long as an hour. She removed the tube and took the oxygen tank, leaving us alone with our baby dressed in white.

We sat close together and held Ammon. He seemed to me to look like an angel, so perfect and peaceful. It was only moments later that we heard what sounded like a tiny gasp. We both knew that his spirit had left his body. Our sweet little baby had died. I thought that perhaps he was impatient with us for taking two days to finally make up our minds, that he had many things he needed to attend to and just couldn't wait any longer.

Both of us cried. I had never seen my husband cry before, but he lay on my bed and sobbed. He had been so stalwart and supportive over the past two days. Now suddenly he was breaking down. Our little baby had really died. There had been no miraculous recovery, and now there was no turning back. I felt so young and helpless, like the little nine-year-old girl who, years before, had peered at her baby brother's body lying in a casket and wondered why she, of all the little girls in the world, had to be the one to feel such heartache. It didn't make sense that this would happen again, I thought. I had already experienced enough sorrow for one life.

The nurses left us alone with Ammon for a few hours. We spent the time rocking his body, singing to him, and reading to him about the prophet Ammon from the Book of Mormon. Even though we knew that he was no longer alive, we hoped that his spirit had remained near us during this time as we tried to share a lifetime of love with our little son in the few short hours that we had with him. We took several pictures, wanting to capture as many memories as we could. Those hours that we spent cradling our little son's body were among the most blessed, reverent, even sacred moments of our lives, a time we will always treasure—being alone with our son, witnessing the peace of his passing, and cradling him in our arms.

When the nurse came back into the room, she took several pictures of Ammon that the hospital later gave us as a gift. James and I each held and kissed him one last time. Then she took him from my room. Completely exhausted from the experience, James and I went to sleep. A few hours later the nurse quietly woke me up, saying that someone from the hospital morgue had come to get Ammon's body, and she wondered if I'd like to see him one last time. After thinking about it, I told her no, that I had already said good-bye. I feared that seeing him now in what I imagined would be a blue and stiff state would detract from the sacred hours that we had spent with him. She told me that after Ammon was taken from our room, a nurse had been holding him while I slept. "I just thought that would comfort you," she said, "to know that he was being held." Through tears I told her that it did.

I didn't see my son's body again while we were in the hospital. When I was released to return home, his body was still in the hospital's morgue. James's dad later made a seven-hour drive to pick up his body and bring it to James's hometown in Wyoming, where he would be buried. As we drove home from Denver, I looked out the window and watched the scenery speed by. Normally I would have enjoyed its beauty, but instead I resented it. My baby was dead. Nothing else mattered to me. We were driving home, but to what? A house full of baby clothes, a cradle, and a car seat that we no longer had any need for? I just wanted to climb into my bed and wait for my heart to stop hurting.

We arrived home to a house full of flowers and a note that meals would be brought in by ward members. I didn't want to see anyone though. I wanted to be left alone. I realized that the members of my ward loved me and wanted to help, but none of them could bring back my baby, and that was all I wanted. Each night I went to sleep hoping I would wake up from this bad dream. Each morning I woke up disappointed.

After a couple of days at home, we drove the nine hours to James's parents' home, where we met our family to have a viewing and graveside service for Ammon.

James and I went to the funeral home to see Ammon's body the night before his viewing. He looked completely different from the baby we had held at the hospital. Even with makeup, he looked dark and rigid. I was asked if I wanted to hold him, and I declined. This body lying in the little casket was not my baby. I didn't want to touch him. I was so bothered by it that I wished I had never seen him that way—yet I knew that if I hadn't, I would have always wished I had. It was a painful, no-win situation. I wished so much that everyone could have seen Ammon living, because this little body lying stiff and blue just wasn't him. I was tempted to cancel the viewing altogether, but I realized that my loved ones were also grieving for my baby and that seeing him might help them to begin healing.

We didn't attend the viewing, and we were among the last to arrive for the graveside service. Our relatives and a small number of friends were in attendance. There were several chairs lined up in front of Ammon's little casket. James's mother had bought a beautiful little floral spray that was draped over Ammon's casket. Several others brought flowers as well, placing them all around his casket and on the green carpet that covered his final resting place. The sky was beautiful and blue. It was summertime, and there were probably birds singing. Children throughout town were probably running through sprinklers and licking popsicles. All of this escaped my notice, however, because all that mattered to me was the baby I no longer had.

A member of James's parents' bishopric conducted the service, and my dad spoke for a few minutes. James's dad sang "Each Life That Touches Ours for Good," and my aunts and a cousin sang "A Baby Dressed in White." It was a beautiful service, with loving words and lovely music. James, strong and stalwart as ever, dedicated Ammon's grave and pronounced a beautiful blessing upon him and our family. After the service ended everyone took turns giving us hugs. Then it was over.

James and I drove around the cemetery until we were sure everyone else had left, then we went back to Ammon's grave site. We saw a cemetery employee using a machine to pound the dirt in over Ammon's grave. It resembled a jackhammer that street workers would use to cut a hole in pavement. He was aware of our sudden presence and seemed almost apologetic that he was performing his duty—something that I hadn't ever considered being done—to cover the grave of our precious baby.

Before returning to Moab with our boys, we visited the cemetery again. The grass had been replaced, but the outline of the grave remained, evidence that our baby was indeed under the ground despite the stretch of green trying to hide it. The baby whose lively kicks, hiccups, and movements had brought me so much joy for seven-and-a-half months was officially gone. I hated to leave him there in the Wyoming ground, so far away from us, where I would not be able to visit his grave regularly. I wished I could just stay there beside him, but I had two little boys to raise. I knew it was time to go home and resume as normal a life as possible for my living children.

Upon arriving home, James returned to his work duties. I mostly just stayed home with the boys. The Relief Society president visited me and expressed the love and concern of the sisters in our ward. Wanting to be alone and yet realizing their need to care for me, I wrote them a letter and gave it to the Relief Society president to read to them. I expressed my love for them and explained what had happened and how we were healing, both physically and emotionally. The Relief Society president shared it with the sisters and told me afterward that everyone had cried. I knew they loved me, and I knew they were hurting for me and my family, but I still did not want to see them. I wanted to be at home with my sons and my husband to deal with my grief privately.

A couple of days after we returned home from Wyoming, my aunt called to tell me that she and her family were in town "on vacation" and wondered if there was anything she could do for me. My extended family was not excluded from my desire for seclusion. I didn't want to see anyone, and that included my beloved aunt. At first I told her no, but I realized she had driven a very long way just to pretend to be on vacation, so I suggested that she might help clean the house. She happily agreed and quickly arrived from her hotel. Trying to avoid having to see or talk to her, I went in the bathroom and took a long bubble bath. I took advantage of the opportunity away from my boys to have a good cry. I felt great relief after crying. However, I realized I didn't want my young boys to remember me constantly crying, so I tried to do it privately whenever possible. When my bath was over, my aunt was gone and my house was spotless. I felt guilty for not visiting with her, giving her a hug, or thanking her for her selfless service, but I was so grateful that she had respected my need for privacy. She had not been pushy or overbearing, but she wanted to serve me and was grateful that I had provided her with something that truly needed to be done—something that I did not have the energy to do myself.

By the time two weeks had passed since Ammon's death, two of my friends thought that I'd been home long enough. One night they arrived unexpectedly at my house, telling me they were kidnapping me for ice cream. Reluctantly, I went with them, but I was miserable the whole time. Although I realized what they were trying to do and appreciated them for it, I was not ready yet to be social. I wished I had just been left at home. I did not feel like answering questions or talking about my experience over and over again. It was like repeatedly reliving it. I was so relieved when they brought me home—I felt safe there.

I didn't attend church for a month. I used my physical condition as an excuse, but the truth was that I was hiding, not wanting to see or talk to anyone. I didn't want to see their sympathetic eyes. I didn't want to answer any questions or share any of my experience. I didn't want to risk crying in front of any of them. My calling at the time was a Sunday School teacher for the sixteen- and seventeen-year-olds. I asked a friend to substitute in the class until I was ready to come back. During my month at home, the bishop released me from this calling and extended a call as the Primary pianist. I was relieved to have a calling that required no talking, where I would draw very little attention to myself. One night a couple of the girls in my Sunday School class brought me a plate of cookies; I gave them each a hug and thanked them for it. After they left I looked at the plate of cookies and realized I had let them down. I have since wished that I had not neglected my Sunday School class during that time. I realized that these young men and women were learning more from me than what was written in our manual. They were watching the way I lived, and watching me grieve may have helped them during their own times of grief later in life.

One of the sisters I visit taught had recently had a baby. She was my good friend, but I dreaded the thought of visiting her home, where I would see or hear her baby—or at the very least, know that he was there. I was tempted to call the Relief Society president and ask her to remove my friend from my visiting teaching route. I felt petty and selfish and wished I had the strength to just keep a stiff upper lip and fulfill my responsibilities. Still, I knew that it would be unfair to my friend to leave her with a visiting teacher who was not capable of meeting her needs as a new mother while I tried to work through my own grief. Finally, I worked up the courage to call the Relief Society president. She revealed to me that my friend had already called her. She had sensed that I would feel uncomfortable being around her new baby and had asked that my visiting teaching route be altered to not include her. I was so grateful for my perceptive friend and my understanding Relief Society president. They were right that being around new babies only reminded me of Ammon. I didn't want to hold them. I didn't want to see them. I didn't want to hear about them.

Within a couple of months, five of my six sisters-in-law were all pregnant. For the most part, they were very sensitive and careful not to talk about their pregnancies in front of me, but I still thought about it all the time. I felt so jealous of them that they would soon have live, healthy babies. And as each of these healthy babies was born, I felt angry at them. Why were they given healthy babies when I wasn't? Did Heavenly Father love them more than He loved me? How could I avoid being around these new babies for the rest of my life so that I wouldn't constantly be reminded of Ammon? At times I felt consumed by anger. I was angry at every mother who complained about her crying baby or sleepless nights. I was angry at the drug-abusing and alcoholic birth mothers of the foster children who came into my home. They had been so selfish and careless during their pregnancies yet had given birth to live babies who at least had a chance at life—the chance that Ammon didn't get. It wasn't fair!

Around this time my husband and I left on a business trip to Tennessee. I thought it would be a much-needed escape from the many reminders of the baby I had lost. During our flight, we overheard a screaming baby and an exasperated, complaining mother. I leaned over to James and whispered that I would gladly trade her screaming baby for a headstone in Wyoming. Realizing the coldness of my comment, I felt very guilty for the way I felt—but I truly felt that way. How dare this woman complain about this priceless gift that she had and I did not?

We had made our reservations months before and didn't think to check on any of the details before arriving. When we checked in at the front desk of our hotel, the clerk asked, "And you'd like one crib?" We looked at each other bewildered. "No," we told her, "we don't need a crib." It was just another reminder of our loss.

A small blessing came to us that day. Instead of the tiny hotel room that we should have been given on this business trip, someone had made arrangements for us to have a presidential suite on the top floor at the same cost. To this day, we still don't know who arranged that gift for us. We spent those few days in luxury amidst lavish furnishings and surroundings that brought us a much-needed reprieve from the realities of home. I was suddenly grateful that the hotel clerk had asked first about the crib rather than having me enter our beautiful hotel suite to find a crib waiting—an empty crib that symbolized our empty hearts and the pain we had suffered over the past few months.

As my anger subsided over time, doubts began to fill my mind. Even with all the confirmations that we had made the right choice, that we had been blessed to have things work out the way they did, I continued to question our decision to disconnect Ammon's life support. I wondered what would have happened if we'd chosen not to. What if we'd given him one more day? Had we killed our son? I spent many sleepless nights lying awake wondering, "What if?" Finally, about six months after Ammon's death, I got out of bed at 1:00 AM and looked through my hospital paperwork. I found the phone number of the hospital and called them, asking for the labor and delivery department. I asked for every nurse whose name I could remember and finally found one that was on duty. I explained who I was and why I was calling. Thankfully, she remembered me. I told her of my doubts and feelings of guilt. I told her of my need to know that we had made the right choice. Understanding and kind, she told me that she remembered a test being performed on Ammon in which they dropped a tiny bit of water into his ear to see how he would respond. She said that his complete lack of response confirmed to them that he had little, if any, brain activity. No, she told me, he would not have recovered. We had made the right choice. She provided me the comfort I needed on that lonely night.

During the months that followed, I had many good days mixed with bad ones. After several months I was able to participate in social events without fearing that I would fall apart at any reminder of Ammon. My boys kept me busy, and I was grateful for that. DCFS continued to place foster children in our home, and that also kept me occupied. Being busy was one of my survival mechanisms. I found that as the months passed I was having more and more happy days and fewer bad ones. All the while I was searching for answers. I had always believed that everything in life happens for a reason. Now I needed to know the reason for Ammon's being taken. I pleaded with Heavenly Father to give me a glimpse into the "big picture" and see Ammon's role in it. I felt I could not accept Ammon's being gone unless there was a logical reason for his absence.

Getting pregnant again helped me to deal with my grief. This time I did not become pregnant easily, however. While I'd been able to conceive within the first month of trying with my first three pregnancies, it took me six months to conceive after Ammon died. My doctor had warned me to wait three months so that I would be emotionally ready to have another baby, but I didn't want to wait at all. It wasn't that I thought a new baby would take Ammon's place. For me, being pregnant meant that

I had something to look forward to, that I had another chance at motherhood, and that I had something to occupy my mind other than the baby I missed so desperately.

When I finally did become pregnant again, I was overwhelmingly happy. It was such a relief to know that I had another chance. I still missed Ammon, but I was so thankful to have another baby on the way.

A couple of months before Ammon's first birthday, DCFS called and asked me to take three-month-old twins. I happily agreed, and these babies were soon brought to my home. We were aware that these babies might eventually be available for adoption, and I wondered if this might be the answer I was searching for. This proved to be true, and later, when they were eighteen months old, we adopted our twins and had them sealed to us. I realized that if Ammon had been alive, DCFS would never have placed our twins with us—the rule was that there could only be two children under the age of two in a home at a time. With an infant of our own at home, we would have been over the limit, and they had to make an exception just for my pregnancy. We truly felt that our twins were meant to be in our family. While we never would have chosen to give up Ammon in exchange for the twins, Heavenly Father had provided a way for us to have all of them—Ammon and the twins—as part of our eternal family.

Ammon's first birthday was very hard. Even though the twin babies kept my arms full and my expanding tummy brought me hope for the future, I still missed Ammon terribly. All of the emotions that I'd felt over the past year came back again on that single day—the anger, the sadness, the worry, and the guilt. Afterward my husband and I decided that Ammon would not want us to spend his birthday feeling sad. He would want us to remember and honor him, but in a positive way. We instituted "Ammon Days," a yearly celebration held around his birthday in which we would do something we think he would have enjoyed if he'd been here. This has become our tradition, and it's something that the family looks forward to all year long.

My acceptance of Ammon's death came little by little. Not until after his first birthday did I fully believe that life was still going to be full of happiness. I would always miss Ammon and wish that he were here, but I would enjoy my other children and the events in my life. Life would continue to go on. I would continue to grow and learn, and it was okay to be happy. That is what Ammon would have wanted.

THREE

Kija

DURING THE YEARS THAT FOLLOWED Ammon's loss, I was blessed with three healthy children—Jamey, Teancum, and the daughter I had longed for, Rebecca. Our large family with seven living children brought us immeasurable happiness, but James and I did not feel that our family was complete. Because of complications during Rebecca's delivery, my doctor had cautioned me about the danger of delivering another baby. I had bled uncontrollably, and he feared I might bleed to death if I had another C-section.

I decided to visit a hematologist, hoping that she would discover that I had some kind of treatable blood disorder and could safely deliver another baby with the proper treatment for my hypothetical condition. After the doctor found nothing and declared me perfectly normal and healthy, James and I were left with a difficult decision about the family we felt was not yet complete. Did we risk my life to have another child? We decided to make it a matter of fasting and prayer.

During our fast, James gave me a priesthood blessing in which he promised me that I would know for certain what I should do. Before our fast was over, I knew that I should have another baby followed by a scheduled hysterectomy to prevent any unforeseen complications. I called my doctor the next day. He agreed with my decision but advised that he would send me to Salt Lake for the delivery, just in case any complications or emergencies occurred. I accepted his decision. A couple of months later I was pregnant.

There were many other pregnant women in our small town at the time, a baby boom that I deemed unusual and which included several of my friends. I remember thinking on more than one occasion that certainly the chances were that all of us wouldn't make it through our pregnancies without some major occurrence. In the back of my mind, I felt that I would be the one whose pregnancy wouldn't go as planned, but I pushed that thought aside and determined that all would be well. After all, Heavenly Father had clearly told me to have this baby, so why would He take her from me?

Physically, my pregnancy was normal, and I felt great. I was able to run a few miles every morning, I ate what I felt like eating, and I did what I felt like doing. I did have more morning sickness than I'd had in previous pregnancies, but I saw this as a good sign. While I was very tired, I was also very happy. I had come to the decision that this was my last child. I was at peace with that and was trying to enjoy every moment of this last pregnancy.

At eight weeks I saw my baby on ultrasound, a perfect little embryo developing normally and beautifully. While I was thrilled that my pregnancy appeared to be going smoothly, I was also uneasy because many nights I woke from dreams that my baby had died. I spent the first part of my pregnancy feeling worried and anxious.

When my sixteenth week of pregnancy arrived, I visited the doctor and heard my baby's heartbeat for the first time. Hearing the heartbeat assuaged my worries. Because of the complications from my last delivery, I had kept this pregnancy a secret from my family and friends. Hearing the heartbeat made me feel like I had finally exited the danger zone, and this gave me the courage I needed to move forward with the announcement of my pregnancy. Shortly after sixteen weeks, I began feeling movement from my baby. I was thrilled beyond words.

At nineteen weeks, I ran a 5K race. I didn't do as well as I would have liked, but I was proud of myself for being able to run despite my now-protruding belly. Shortly after the race, our family left on a fun-filled vacation to Rapid City, South Dakota. It was our "Ammon Days" celebration, an especially important one because this would have been Ammon's eighth birthday celebration. For the first time in my pregnancy, I was wearing maternity clothes. I relished the opportunity to show off my growing belly. I was a proud pregnant mama who had just barely made the grand announcement. Everyone seemed to be genuinely happy for us, although some admitted to being worried about my safety. I assured them that all would be well. I felt that this pregnancy was a partnership with Heavenly Father and that He would watch over me throughout it.

We returned from our trip excited about our next adventure—the birth of our ninth child. Only two days after our return, we all piled into our fifteen-passenger van and headed to the doctor's office to find out if we were having a baby brother or a baby sister. The children were all giddy with anticipation. While I secretly hoped for a little sister for Rebecca, I mostly just wanted a healthy baby for the caboose of our family. But it was Rebecca's second birthday, and she definitely deserved a sister! After all, her brothers were very poor companions at tea parties, and they just didn't understand why it was necessary to bring an extra pair of shoes along to every destination, just in case a change in style was needed.

Our doctor entered the room, which had probably surpassed its occupancy limit by several kids, and started the ultrasound. I could see the concern on his face as he looked at our baby on the monitor. After first measuring the head and mentioning that it was measuring small, he moved to the chest. I could see for myself that the heart was still. My heart, too, went still that day as I saw my motionless baby whom I'd already felt life from, and for whom I had such high hopes and dreams.

My doctor started to talk in a hushed whisper so that only James and I could hear what he was saying. He told us that our baby appeared to be a girl and that she measured at about sixteen weeks. I was shocked and couldn't understand what the doctor was saying. I had heard my baby's heartbeat at sixteen weeks. That was weeks ago when I finally felt safe telling people. There had to be some mistake! I started to ask my doctor for an explanation, but he said that he just didn't know what had gone wrong. Sometimes, he said, we never know.

Soon my older children realized what was happening. I could see the look of fear in their faces. The younger children, not understanding what the doctor was saying, began to get restless. "Is it a boy or a girl?" one of my boys asked. "I want to see the baby," Rebecca said. My doctor looked at me, not wishing to say more with my children in the room. He told me that he would leave us alone for as long as we needed and that he would call me after I got home. After he left, James and I calmly explained to our children that our baby girl was not alive. The tears didn't start to flow until after we arrived home. I was grateful that Rebecca was only two years old so that she wouldn't remember how sad and distracted her parents were on her birthday. As she blew out the candles on her birthday cake, I thought of my other little girl who would never get to blow out candles. How could this happen again?

Because of my prior bleeding problems, delivery of the stillborn was an issue. A C-section would almost definitely lead to excessive bleeding and a hysterectomy, as could a D&C, a procedure otherwise known as dilation and curettage, in which the cervix is dilated and the uterus is scraped to clean out the womb. After our doctor consulted with the physicians in Salt Lake, they decided on a VBAC, or vaginal birth after caesarean. This meant that I would not have to undergo surgery at all—I could deliver vaginally. We made plans for the delivery, and our family once again climbed into our van, this time to drive five hours to Salt Lake, where the doctors would induce labor and our tiny daughter would be born. During our long drive, James and I silently cried. I prayed that it wouldn't be true—maybe the machine had malfunctioned and the doctors in Salt Lake would discover that all was well with my baby. The sinking feeling in my heart, however, told me this wouldn't happen.

I spent a sleepless night at my parents' house in Bountiful before the scheduled procedure. I kept thinking that I could still feel my baby move. I lay on my stomach with my hands underneath me and concentrated, hoping for confirmation that this had all just been a big mistake. I thought that maybe if I prayed hard enough, Heavenly Father would provide the miracle that we hadn't received with Ammon. This time our baby would be fine. *Our baby would be fine!*

The next morning we left the kids with my parents while we went to the hospital to deliver our baby. The nurses were expecting me and quickly ushered me to a room at the end of the hall. I noticed the plaque outside the door and realized that we were being placed in the "special room"—the room reserved for parents who wouldn't be bringing babies home from the hospital. Entering the room felt almost like I was adding finality to my situation—perhaps if I requested a different room I would receive a different outcome. Perhaps if I just turned around and went home right now I wouldn't ever have to face the painful hours that I knew lay ahead of me.

As soon as the nurse offered me a gown, I requested another ultrasound—just to be sure. I explained that I thought I had continued to feel the baby move during the night, and I wondered if there had been some sort of mistake with my doctor's equipment. This was my seventh pregnancy and surely I could not mistake the movements of my unborn baby. I felt embarrassed admitting that I doubted my baby's death, but I certainly didn't want to risk an early delivery of a live baby that would have been fine had labor not been induced. Much to my surprise, the nurse quickly agreed. She brought the ultrasound machine into my room.

The ultrasound was performed by the head resident and had the same result as the previous one from my doctor. I asked her to look all over my uterus, because maybe there was a twin hiding in there somewhere. Without making me feel foolish, she checked my entire uterus again but still had the same sad news: there was one baby in there, and that baby was not alive.

Several hours passed while I waited to be induced. It was a weekend, a time when the nursing staff was short. Finally it was determined that an epidural would be placed first, and then labor would be induced. At last the anesthesiologist arrived and the most physically painful part of my experience was taken care of—the placing of the epidural. Labor started rapidly and I progressed rather quickly. My parents brought the kids to visit me in the hospital. The company of my living, vibrant children was the best medicine I could have received.

The nurses told us that some parents whose babies died before birth had allowed their children to meet the baby after it was born. Some of our boys had asked to see the baby. We felt this could be a way to help them heal. I knew that if my younger children didn't physically see her, they might doubt that she had ever really existed. The head resident warned us, however, that the baby's appearance might be disturbing to the children. We determined that this was a decision we could not make until we had seen the baby ourselves. We told my parents to keep the children awake in case we decided to let them meet her.

The hours continued to pass, however, and nothing was happening. I was fully dilated, but the baby was not coming out. They didn't want me to push, because they didn't want to damage the baby's body or put me in any danger. My unique situation caused all of the staff concern, and no one wanted to cause any problems by acting too quickly. I could feel that the baby was partially out, but they didn't want to pull her the rest of the way for fear that the placenta wouldn't immediately follow. Then they might have to scrape my uterus, possibly causing bleeding problems. I lay in agony all night long, feeling my baby's body in the birth canal and not being able to do anything about it.

At some point during the night, a lab technician came to take a blood sample. While she was there, the on-call doctor entered the room and introduced himself. I had so many questions I wanted to ask him, but as soon as I started to talk I was instantly sobbing. I could tell that the lab tech was very uncomfortable and was hurrying as quickly as she could so that she could leave my room. The doctor also appeared to not know how to deal with my sudden outburst. I asked him for a box of tissues and then began asking questions. "Why did I continue to get bigger even after the baby had died?" "Why did I still feel her move if she was dead?" Why, why, why? He explained that even though my baby had died, my placenta continued to grow and my body continued to create more amniotic fluid. He said that I may have been feeling my baby's body floating around in the fluid and hitting the sides of my uterus. As he answered my questions, I could sense how uncomfortable he was. He soon left as quickly as he had come. I listened to my husband sleep, but I lay awake all night.

Finally, at 5:00 AM the head resident and a nurse came to my room. The resident asked me to push while she gently pulled my baby out. So at twenty weeks and one day gestation, my baby was born. The most amazing thing to me was the date of her birth—one day before Ammon's eighth birthday and two days before the eighth anniversary of his death. What an interesting coincidence for their births and deaths to fall so close together. I felt that it was a blessing—another way for us to remember them, and for them, the two members of our family beyond the veil, to be together.

The resident placed my baby on a small blanket and quickly arranged her for me to see. She had warned me how the baby might look, but I was not prepared for what I saw. I first asked her, "Is it a boy or a girl?" She looked at my baby for a few seconds and then said, "I think it's a boy."

Then the nurse handed me my baby and asked what we would name him. I said, "Johnathon Lehi," and then she and the head resident left us alone. He had the appearance of a Barbie doll and was about the same size, although his head was bigger. It had, however, been compressed and misshapen either during delivery or during his lifeless time before birth. One of his eyes was open, revealing what looked like a translucent piece of glass. I looked at his sexual organs, and, while they appeared peculiar, I did not doubt the head resident's determination of his sex. I had no medical training so I trusted her judgment. His tiny hands and feet were perfect, with separated fingers and toes—ten of each. I reverently looked at him as I held him in my hands. I didn't understand why his body had stopped working—it looked so perfect and complete. There was no sign of distress. There were no clues that would help us understand what had happened.

We decided that because of our baby's appearance, particularly his misshapen head and blue pallor, we did not want our children to see him. Instead of remembering him this way, we wanted them to imagine him as a normal baby—the cute, chubby ones they saw all around town. The nursing staff offered to give him a bath, take pictures of him, and make molds of his hands and feet for us to keep. We agreed that this suggestion was what we wanted.

They took pictures of his hands and feet only, none of his face or body. They told us we could keep him with us as long as we wanted to, and they also gave us the decision of how to dispose of his body. We could have him cremated and would be given his ashes to keep or scatter, or we could make arrangements for his burial.

A nurse who had herself delivered a baby at fifteen weeks told us that she'd chosen to have her baby cremated. She explained the procedure and described how she'd picked up her baby's ashes in a pretty little box with a bow. We were leaning toward cremation when we received a phone call and news of a very kind funeral home owner who would provide us with a casket and burial services at no charge. We were overwhelmed with gratitude and relief, because somehow the thought of Johnathon's tiny body being burned seemed to me like an added cruelty to the already horrible situation. The nurse came to take Johnathon's body to pathology for an autopsy, and that was the last time we saw him.

Soon the nurses moved me to a room in a different section of the hospital. I was grateful to be taken out of the maternity ward, but I also didn't feel like I fit in with the sick people in other areas of the hospital. I was not in very much physical pain, but I requested an extra night in the hospital because I was not emotionally ready to face my children, or anyone else.

Because of the timing of gestation, my baby's death was considered a stillbirth. If he'd been born two days earlier, before twenty weeks, it would have been considered a miscarriage. The nurse at the hospital explained this to me and then quickly added, "But does it really matter?" No, the terminology did not matter. Either way, my baby was gone.

Because of the vaginal delivery and Johnathon's tiny size, I felt completely normal upon my exit from the hospital. James and I picked up our children from my parents' house and drove home. Aside from some residual soreness at the epidural site, I was completely void of pain. Physically, I didn't even feel as if I had been pregnant, much less delivered a baby. I wore tight sports bras to prohibit my milk from letting down a couple days later when my body started to lactate. My healthy and normal outside appearance certainly did not match the emotional wreck I was on the inside. I felt betrayed by Heavenly Father. I thought we had entered this pregnancy as a partnership, but He had let me down. Why would He give me the distinct impression that I was to have another child, and then take him from me in so cruel a manner—before I'd been able to get to know and enjoy him at all?

We were home only a couple of days before James's dad brought our baby's body to us so that he could be buried next to his older brother Ammon. He met us at our house, the tiny casket in the back of his van, and we all drove up to the cemetery where a grave had been prepared. We let each of the kids hold Johnathon's casket, and we took pictures before James dedicated the grave. Then the children and I went home, James's dad drove back to Evanston, and James went back to work. This time we didn't stay to watch the cemetery staff pound the dirt over his grave. I did, however, return to the cemetery a few hours later and saw the green grass laid back as it had been before, with only the outline of the tiny square revealing the secret it hid below.

I'd been through the grief process before. I knew the experience that lay ahead of me, but I also knew that I would come out of it eventually and feel at peace. Having a knowledge of what I would go through gave me a feeling of control that I didn't have after Ammon's death, so I just waited and let life and my emotions take their course.

I once believed that I would never be able to handle losing a baby. After Ammon died, I learned that Heavenly Father provides us with the strength we need to handle our trials. While I certainly never would have chosen to lose another of my children, I knew from experience that Heavenly Father would help me through my grief.

Because I felt totally normal physically, I asked the ward not to prepare dinners for our family. I felt silly having someone else do something that I could easily do myself. However, my friends still felt the need to help me in some way. Most of my ward members hadn't even realized I was pregnant, so learning of my baby's death was traumatic for the entire ward. Women have a need to nurture—a need to be needed—and my friends needed me to need them at this time.

One day I came upstairs around lunchtime to find my friend putting a pot in my refrigerator. I asked her what she was doing. She gave me a hug, told me that she loved me, and said that I could heat the meal up at dinnertime. For the rest of the week, friends showed up at lunchtime with food to be heated up for dinner. One night a pizza delivery man arrived with pizzas that had already been anonymously paid for. I realized that my friends were searching for ways to share their love with me while at the same time respecting my desire for privacy. The many notes, cards, and e-mails that I received helped me feel loved and comforted during those first difficult weeks and long afterward.

A couple of weeks after we buried Johnathon, I took the kids to visit my family and participate in our annual Jet Ski vacation. As I drove a Jet Ski around the lake with the wind blowing through my hair, I looked up at the sky and the beautiful mountains. I felt the first glimmer of hope and peace that I'd felt since I learned that my tiny baby was dead. I felt Heavenly Father's love envelop me, and for the first time in those few weeks, I felt happy. I knew that I still had a painful grieving process ahead of me, but I silently thanked Heavenly Father for those moments of hope and optimism that He had afforded me. Somewhere in the back of my mind I knew I would need those moments to buoy me up because more heartache still lay ahead.

Nearly a month after Johnathon's birth, I was ready to send in my payment and final paperwork for his headstone. I still had some lingering doubts, so I thought I ought to at least try to learn the results of the autopsy before taking such a large step toward his memorial.

I called my doctor's office and asked if they'd received anything from the Salt Lake hospital related to the autopsy. After several phone calls, the nurse finally received a faxed copy of the autopsy. I asked if it revealed anything about what had caused my baby's death. She replied that it did not but listed her as a normal baby girl. Stunned, I told her there must be some mistake, because the baby I had was a boy—the head resident had told me so! The nurse repeated that the autopsy stated that it was a normal baby girl. I asked to receive a copy of the autopsy, and she consented. I needed to see these words on paper before I would believe them—perhaps she had read them incorrectly.

I started making phone calls to the Salt Lake hospital asking for some sort of explanation. I wanted to know what the results of the genetic testing had been. Had my baby been switched with someone else's? How could my baby look enough like a boy to make even the head resident think it was a boy, but be described as a "normal baby girl"? I talked with several people at the hospital, but no one could give me concrete answers. Finally, I just left them with my cell phone number and went on with my planned events.

I was at my son's baseball game when my cell phone rang. I hurried to the outskirts of the parking lot to answer it. It was the head of the pathology department. He apologized for the misunderstanding and mishandling of my case. He told me that he'd obtained a copy of my baby's cytogenetic screening, which had just barely been completed. It confirmed that I'd had a "normal female baby." He explained that the head resident had probably been mistaken because of the early gestation of my baby—at the early stage of development when she was delivered, it was just difficult to tell. The autopsy measurements didn't give us any indication of what caused her death, but they did provide us with a better timeline. The doctor estimated that, according to her measurements, she had died around eighteen weeks' gestation.

To say that I was in shock would be a gross understatement. I'd lived for a month believing I'd lost a boy, had told all of our family and friends that we'd lost a boy, and now suddenly it was as if we'd lost a completely different baby. I had created an image of Johnathon in my mind, and he'd become a very real person to me. Now I pictured three children that I had lost— Ammon, Johnathon, and now this new baby girl. It took a long time before I reconciled my memories to coincide with the birth of a daughter instead of the birth of a son. The first thing we did was visit the cemetery and rededicate the grave, this time for Kija Marin, our daughter.

How to tell people was another problem. What if they thought my baby was malformed or horrifyingly disfigured? How would we explain why we had thought it was a boy when it was really a girl? Could we keep it a secret and just let them believe we had lost a boy? What if they visited the cemetery and saw Kija's name on the headstone? And what on earth should we tell our children?

I decided that the most efficient way to let people know of the misunderstanding was to place an obituary in the local newspaper. I sent out birth announcements, making no mention of Johnathon Lehi but only talking about our daughter Kija. We also sent an e-mail to our family members letting them know of the situation. I changed the name on the drawings for Kija's headstone and sent the payment in.

James suggested that it was much better to find out this way than to get to heaven and be surprised to discover that we had a daughter waiting for us. While I was relieved to finally know the truth and feel some finality, I started the grieving process all over again. I couldn't simply forget Johnathon, and yet he was now just a fictional character whom I had created. And I felt like I'd been cheated out of the opportunity to get to know Kija because during those hours that we had spent with our baby, we thought she was Johnathon. Once again I felt like Heavenly Father had dealt me a harsh blow. I didn't understand what I had done to deserve so much heartache in my life. I feared what might still lie in store for me. When would Heavenly Father decide I had suffered enough?

My anger toward God was not short-lived. My husband admitted to being worried about me because some nights I even refused to pray with him, making the comment that God wouldn't listen to me anyway. Secretly, however, I was praying all the time. I was praying for answers and understanding. I was praying for comfort and peace. And I was praying that I would never again have to feel so much pain.

A couple of months before Kija's delivery, a friend and I had committed to give four other expectant moms a baby shower. Although it was soon after Kija's death, I felt that I needed to honor that commitment. I just didn't know if I had the strength to face these moms whose physical appearance showed that they had what had been taken from me. I did not feel at all ready to enjoy social events—especially a baby shower—but I remembered my regrets after losing Ammon. I decided I needed to be less selfish this time. I needed to serve others and forget my own feelings of sadness for awhile. My friend and I planned the shower and many people came. It was an enjoyable evening, but when it was time to go home, the four women gathered for a group picture. As I looked over at them, a lump formed in my throat. I thought, *I should be standing with them. This isn't fair.* My best intentions to forget myself for a night had failed. I hurried as quickly as I could to clean up and escape for home before the tears started to fall.

Kija's original due date soon neared, and I'd just reached the point where I was participating in the activities that I had enjoyed before. I was finally able to be out in public without feeling like I might fall apart at any time. One of the first social events I attended after I reached this point was the broadcast of the annual general Relief Society meeting. The theme they had chosen for the year was "Encircled Eternally in the Arms of His Love." Repeatedly, a picture of a newborn baby cradled in his mother's arms was shown on the screen. I was grateful that we were seated in a dark room where only my friend next to me noticed that tears were streaming down my face. I realized the beauty of the message being shared, but the picture of the newborn baby was too much for me to bear. I thought I could handle being out again, but I just couldn't keep it together any longer. I should be the mother holding that baby, I thought. That should have been *me!*

The next day was fast Sunday in our ward. I felt that I would be able to control my emotions and that the previous night's outburst would not be relived. I sat near the back of the chapel with my large family and enjoyed the meeting. Near the end, a man whose family had recently moved into the ward approached the microphone to share his testimony. His wife was among the many pregnant women in our community. She would soon deliver their third child. He expressed his anxiety over the thought of having three young children to care for. Then he suddenly said, "But you can't return them!" Everybody laughed. Everybody, that is, except me. My ward family, whom I had always felt such love and acceptance from, now felt like a room of strangers to me. I felt completely alone. I knew that this man's comment was innocent, that he had moved in after we lost Kija, and that he had no idea of our situation. But, unfortunately, sometimes babies are returned to Heavenly Father—and at that moment I decided that I was the only one who understood that. The tears started to well up in my eyes, and I knew I wouldn't be able to control them. I picked up Rebecca, walked out the back door of the chapel, out of the church, and straight home.

Of all the days to lock my doors, that had to be the one, and I didn't have my keys with me. I sat on the steps in our garage, held Rebecca tight, and cried. I let it all out—all the anger, all the jealousy, all the despair—it all poured out in my tears. I was completely exhausted from trying to hold my emotions in. I was so tired of pretending I wasn't still hurting. I couldn't continue to be strong. I was just too tired.

A small miracle occurred that day. Because of our callings, James and I usually would not see each other at all for the last two hours of church. He had been sitting on the other end of our pew and hadn't realized that I had gone home. During Sunday School he had the prompting that he should come looking for me. When the other members of the Primary presidency told him that I had not come to Primary that day, he knew something was wrong. He hurried home and found me huddled with Rebecca in the garage. He didn't have his keys either, but he was able to climb through a window to let us into the house. He sat with me on the couch, his arms around me, and let me cry. I am so grateful to have an understanding husband who perceived that I needed him that day and followed the prompting to be there for me.

The ironic part about this situation was that the healthy baby daughter of the man who bore his testimony was born within a week of Kija's due date. She was given a name that rhymed with Kija, and she was their third child. I couldn't help but think of my third child, Ammon, and how things had turned out so much differently for him. I spent the next year avoiding this family because every time I saw their daughter, I thought of Kija. Then one day this mother told me that before she'd given birth to her three healthy daughters, she had experienced five miscarriages. I had completely misjudged the situation. This woman, whom I had avoided for a year, could have been offering me comfort and guidance during my own time of grief, but I had been pushing her away.

I had been trying ever since Kija's stillbirth to get pregnant again. Just as after Ammon, things were not happening as quickly as I hoped they would. I went to see my doctor. He ran some tests that revealed that I had polycystic ovarian syndrome—a hormone problem that often causes either temporary or long-term infertility. Though I have no medical basis, I wonder if the same was true after Ammon died. I also suspect—again, with no medical knowledge of my own—that because I didn't nurse Ammon and Kija, my hormones behaved differently than they did after giving birth to my living children and therefore contributed to the difficulties with getting pregnant. So I continued to wait. After five months, I did become pregnant again, but I was reluctantly relieved. I had already lost two babies. Who could promise me that this pregnancy would not have the same result?

While I had always enjoyed running regularly, after I lost Kija I didn't feel like running anymore. I felt guilty that I had been running during my pregnancy with her, and even though my doctor told me that running had not caused her death, I still wondered. When I became pregnant again, I did not run. I didn't even go on walks very often. I tried to do everything just the opposite of how I had handled things during Kija's pregnancy. I announced my pregnancy immediately and began wearing maternity clothes right away. Every question of "What if . . . ?" that I had experienced after Kija's death I tried to make up for during my next pregnancy—as if getting it right this time would save this baby's life. I wondered if Kija had somehow felt unwelcome because I had kept her pregnancy a secret. I didn't want to risk that happening again.

I also wondered if Kija had looked down on our family and decided that she did not want to be part of this rough-and-tumble crew or that she didn't want me for a mother. I expressed these thoughts to my stake president. He helped me understand how false they were. Children do not simply leave because they know their parents are in any way unfit—otherwise drug addicts, abusive parents, or pedophiles would never have children, but we all know this happens. But if I couldn't blame myself for what happened, then who could I blame? It had to be someone's fault. I also expressed to my stake president my feelings of anger toward God. I was feeling overwhelmed with guilt because I felt so angry at my Heavenly Father, the one who had given me my life and everything I held dear yet had also allowed things that I held dear to be taken from me, especially my two children. I knew that He loved me, and I knew He knew what was best for me. But I wanted Him to do things *my* way! I had planned out my life the way I knew it should occur, and I was frustrated that God had not followed *my* plan.

Always wanting to know the reasons behind things, I pleaded with Heavenly Father for understanding. Because our twins had joined our family, I could see more of the "big picture" in Ammon's case, but what about this time? My husband was now a prosecuting attorney for the county, so we were no longer eligible to be foster parents. DCFS would not be calling us to place children that we could later adopt. Why did we have to lose Kija? I thought about the hysterectomy that I had planned in combination with Kija's birth. If I had followed through with this hysterectomy, I would not have been able to get pregnant again and would never have had this new baby that was on the way. But why couldn't I have both of them? Why couldn't I have carried Kija to term and delivered her safely without bleeding problems so that a hysterectomy wouldn't be needed? Why did things have to happen this way? It was several months before I accepted the fact that I would probably never know *why* during this life. As my doctor had told me, sometimes we just never know.

By the time Kija's first birthday came and we made preparations for "Ammon and Kija Days," I was ready to move on with my life and allow myself to feel happy again. There are still nights when I lie awake thinking about both Ammon and Kija. While we do not have doctrine defining when the spirit enters a fetus, I feel strongly, and it comforts me to believe, that the spirit enters earlier rather than later—and that, therefore, Kija has a spirit. I have often wondered how much influence she and Ammon have in my life right now. They are probably both very busy with other things, but I wonder if every now and then they look in on our family and long to share the love they feel for us.

FOUR

_This Doesn't Happen to Me

> "While he spake these things unto them, behold,
> there came a certain ruler, and worshipped him,
> saying, My daughter is even now dead: but come
> and lay thy hand upon her, and she shall live."
>
> —Matthew 9:18

THE LATE ELISABETH KÜBLER-ROSS, M.D., became one of the most world-renowned experts on death and grief over the course of her career. Her now-famous Five Stages of Grief were the topic of many of my social work courses at Brigham Young University. The stages made sense to me—so much so that I still remembered them in detail many years after my graduation.

After Ammon died, I watched myself, as if through a window, as I progressed through the stages. I found it comical at times to see myself mirror the case studies I had read about and yet seem to have no control to stop the process—perhaps realizing the importance of letting it proceed.

In her book *On Death and Dying*, Kübler-Ross describes the stages of loss from the perspective of a dying person. In *On Grief and Grieving*, a collaborative work with David Kessler, Kübler-Ross follows the stages of loss from the perspective of someone who has lost a loved one. Both books provide valuable insights into the grieving process. Every person is an individual, and each individual grieves in his or her own way. Kübler-Ross states, "Our grief is as individual as our lives" (*On Grief and Grieving*, 7). However, there will be some very important similarities, and understanding them can help us through difficult times.

The first stage of grief is shock or denial. There is little question that when someone is suffering a loss, especially the death of a loved one, they will first deny that it could happen to them. "Everything is fine," or "I'm fine," or "There must be some mistake" are very normal reactions. All of these thoughts entered my mind with the passing of both of my children and the loss of my brother.

With Ammon, my denial was quite obvious in my distinct efforts to ignore what the doctors told me and to cling to the priesthood blessing Ammon had received soon after his birth. The doctors were all wrong, the tests were all wrong; the blessing stated that Ammon would be fine—and he *would* be fine! I denied every piece of medical evidence that would cause me pain because I could not deal with the pain yet.

Once when I was in the NICU visiting Ammon, I was discussing his blood type with the nurse on duty. I was referring to the Rh factor and said that when he got married he would have to be sure to choose a wife with the same blood type as his. The nurse looked at me in surprise and then sheepishly nodded in agreement. As soon as I said it I realized that through my words I was denying the probable outcome. A dying baby has no need to worry about finding a wife, or about how the Rh factor would affect his unborn children, for that matter.

Even after we'd decided to take Ammon off life support, I hoped that when the tubes came out of him he would suddenly let out a cry and miraculously become a normal baby, living and healthy. I was so certain he would prove the doctors wrong. When he breathed his last breath and died, I just couldn't believe it really happened. There must have been some mistake.

The day after Ammon died, a nurse walked in unexpectedly and found me sitting on the edge of my bed with tears running down my face, James's arms around me. She apologized for the intrusion, but later she told me she was grateful to see me cry because she was worried that I might not be fully grasping my son's death. My tears represented to her the end of my denial.

Before Kija's birth, I denied the knowledge that she had died inside me. I still felt her tiny movements even after my doctor showed me her still heart on the ultrasound. After my arrival at the hospital, I asked the nurse to perform another ultrasound because I was certain that my baby was still moving inside me. When the head resident showed me once again my lifeless baby on the screen, I insisted that she thoroughly examine my entire uterus because certainly there was a living twin in there who was alive and well. She showed me an empty abyss of amniotic fluid, simply black on the monitor. There was no other baby there, but I continued to be convinced that I was feeling flutterings for a few weeks after Kija's birth and wondered if I could have delivered a lifeless baby with a twin somehow remaining, still growing and healthy in my womb.

After I learned that Johnathon was a girl, I didn't believe it, and suggested that my baby had been switched with someone else's in the pathology department. There had to be some sort of mistake, because I just *knew* that my baby was a boy. My grief process started completely over that day as I grieved for this seemingly new baby.

Parents who have learned that their child will eventually die may spend quite a long time in this stage. The thought of their child being gone is not something they are ready to accept. Pushing or hurrying them to face reality may result in feelings of resentment on their part. If they are like me, trying to get them to abandon their denial may make them cling more stubbornly to it.

Feelings of denial may serve a valuable purpose because they may be the motivation that parents need to receive the answers they will one day be grateful to have. Running additional tests on a dying infant will bring more reassurance that the parents are making the best choices for their baby. If they simply accept the doctors' initial decision, they may always wonder what might have happened if they had sought a second opinion, run an additional test, or waited a little bit longer.

After Ammon died, the nurses asked if we'd like to have an autopsy done. We declined because we felt that we already knew what had caused his death. I thought an autopsy involved cutting up his body, and I just didn't want that done. After Kija died, I asked a lot of questions and learned that even when a person's body is autopsied, it still remains intact. We chose to have both an autopsy and genetic testing done on Kija's body. We wanted answers. I have since regretted not having an autopsy performed on Ammon because perhaps we could have understood more about his trauma in the womb. Later in the grief process, we find ourselves asking the question, "What if?" Getting the answers while they are available may be a good idea for peace of mind.

Some women who have lost babies early in their pregnancies have admitted to me that they wished they had had autopsies or genetic testing done, but either they didn't know it was available or they declined the option. By the time they changed their mind, it was too late. Then they were left to wonder about the details of their baby's death. After hearing that a larger number of boys than girls are stillborn, I wondered if many of those babies were born early in pregnancy like Kija was, and were simply mistaken for boys.

If you are a loved one of grieving parents, gently persuading them to have available tests run may be helpful to them later on. Because they are in shock, they may not be thinking clearly enough to consider their future feelings. Without being pushy, you may try to explain why searching for answers now could provide peace later.

According to Kübler-Ross, "This first stage of grieving helps us to survive the loss" (*On Grief and Grieving*, 10). This was certainly true in my case. I could not face the truth all at once. I needed to create my own reality as the facts slowly sank in.

FIVE

A *Mother's* Fury

"For she had supposed that we had perished in the wilderness; and she also had complained against my father, telling him that he was a visionary man; saying: Behold thou hast led us forth from the land of our inheritance, and my sons are no more, and we perish in the wilderness. And after this manner of language had my mother complained against my father."

—1 Nephi 5:2–3

THE SECOND STAGE OF GRIEF is anger. As Latter-day Saint women, we are taught to be loving, kind, and patient. We are certainly not taught to be angry. Watching from the outside, a grieving mother's anger may appear as a sign that she is not handling things well, especially if her anger is directed at others. She may react with hostility and possibly cause permanent damage to an otherwise good relationship.

As previously mentioned, over the course of the year after Ammon died, five of my six sisters-in-law had babies. Despite my best intentions, I was very angry at all of them for having healthy babies. I was also angry with any pregnant woman who complained about her pregnancy, or with any young mother who complained about her crying baby or sleepless nights. I wished more than anything for the crying baby and purposeful sleepless nights. I was angry at anyone who complained about having what I could not.

As a foster mother, I felt a great deal of anger toward the birth mothers of my foster children. Many of these women had exposed their unborn children to drugs and alcohol in the womb, but they were blessed with living and, for the most part, healthy babies. I had rarely even taken Tylenol while I was pregnant, but I was not blessed as they were. I was angry that I was the one being punished when, in my view, these women were the ones who deserved punishment.

At the same time, I felt very guilty for my anger because I realized that none of them really deserved it—some were even oblivious to it. I realized my anger was irrational, but a grieving woman is not thinking rationally—or at least not *feeling* rationally. In the case of my sisters-in-law, we all made it through with our relationships still intact, but we might not have if they hadn't been understanding about my anger.

After Kija's passing I wasn't angry at other women; my anger was felt in different ways, directed at different recipients. The major one was God, and I was angry at Him for a long time. I felt as if I had entered into this great plan with Him, and I was angry that He, for some reason, had let me down. I was angry that some people had never lost any babies, while I had lost two. I felt like God had taken away my tiny baby who was never able to enjoy life while there were so many elderly, sick people who had lived a good life and were ready to die. I was especially angry at God after I found out that Johnathon was actually Kija. It wasn't that I loved the baby any less when I thought it was a boy, but after giving birth to five boys in a row before finally having a girl, I saw that girls were rare for me, so why would God allow a rare girl to be taken away? It just wasn't fair, and I told Him all about that.

My angry behavior was not withheld from my husband. One night I angrily blamed him for Kija's death, saying that if only he had given me a priesthood blessing stating that my baby would be healthy and alive, none of this would have happened. Of course, this outburst of anger was really indirectly aimed at God, who I knew only used James as a tool to deliver the priesthood blessings that He had in store for me. Still, with my angry words I was hurting my husband, who himself was grieving over our loss. The one who mattered the most to me in life was also the one who was receiving the greatest amount of fallout from my grief. Thankfully he saw through my blame. With his unconditional love, I was eventually able to let go of my anger. There were many days when James was the *only* person I wanted to talk to. I don't know how I would have made it through the ordeals without him.

Surprisingly, after Kija's death I was also angry at Ammon and Kija, who at that point I thought was Johnathon, because I wanted desperately for them to visit me in spirit form. I pleaded with Heavenly Father to allow just a few seconds of time for me to see my two children, just to know that they were together and doing well in the spirit world. I wanted to know that Ammon was taking care of his younger sibling. I just knew that if only I could see them for a moment then I would be at peace. But they never came. I couldn't understand why they couldn't spare just a few moments for their mother, after I had given them life and been through immense pain on their behalf. Didn't they owe that to me? Now I understand that such spiritual experiences do not occur simply because we want and request them. Such an experience would be extremely rare.

Even as I progressed through the other stages of grief, sometimes my feelings of anger would return. The guilt I felt for my angry feelings would also return because I knew that no one deserved the anger I felt toward them, especially God, who held the master plan over my life. He wanted only to comfort me and provide me the strength I needed to deal with my trials, and yet I was pushing Him away.

Grieving parents who have lost a child by the fault of another have a very obvious person to feel anger toward. MADD (Mothers Against Drunk Drivers) is very aptly named because mothers who have lost a loved one due to the carelessness of a drunk driver are usually very angry. Some grieving parents may feel angry at the doctors who fail to save their child—some parents even file lawsuits against them. Many women are angry at themselves, blaming themselves for their baby's death and wishing they could turn back time and make things happen differently. But if there is no one left to blame, oftentimes the blame falls on God, as in my case.

Expressing your anger is necessary, but taking it out on innocent bystanders—especially your loved ones—will not help you in the long run. You could write openly and honestly about your angry feelings in your journal. Or, if you feel that is still too public, you could write them on a sheet of paper and then throw it away. If you have an understanding friend or family member who will not judge you for your honest feelings, you could express them to her and thus get the anger off your chest. Pretending not to be angry, however, will not help. People who harbor angry feelings often end up expressing them physically—whether it be through ulcers or other stomach complaints, sleep problems, or loss of appetite.

Putting anger to constructive use is another option. I used my anger toward drug-abusing pregnant women as motivation to lobby our state legislators for tougher laws to protect babies from prenatal drug exposure. Giving myself a direction to channel my anger was helpful, especially since I couldn't just make it vanish. It also provided a way to fill my time as I worked through the grief process.

If you are reading this book in the hope of comforting a grieving loved one, keep in mind that they may be in the anger stage of their grief process. They may take their anger out on you, even though you are only trying to help. If you can treat them with patience and realize that their angry feelings will subside, it will help prevent any permanent damage to your relationship. They realize that you love them, but often they just don't know how else to express their anger. Perhaps you are the only one they feel comfortable enough taking it out on—you are the one who will understand.

As part of the grief—and healing—process, our anger also serves an important purpose. Without it, we cannot move on.

We may alarm those around us because we've spent one day writing poems about our baby and then suddenly the next day we're crying out angrily to God. Some may reprimand us for our anger, but holding it in or denying that it exists will only make it worse.

Eventually, my anger faded, but it took longer for my guilty feelings about the anger to subside. Intellectually, I knew that anger was a necessary stage in grieving, but at the same time I felt that I should be above that. I was striving to be a righteous mother, wife, and person, and anger was unbecoming of someone like me. In *On Grief and Grieving*, Kübler-Ross and Kessler state, "Anger affirms that you *can* feel, that you *did* love, and that you *have* lost" (16).

SIX

*W*hat If?

"And she vowed a vow, and said, O Lord of hosts,
if thou wilt indeed look on the affliction of thine
handmaid, and remember me, and not forget
thine handmaid, but wilt give unto thine hand-
maid a man child, then I will give him unto the
Lord all the days of his life . . ."

—1 Samuel 1:11

BARGAINING IS THE THIRD STAGE in the process of grief, and this is one that is often hard to explain in terms of the death of a loved one. When people find out that they are terminally ill, they may bargain with God, saying that if only He will give them more time they will serve the needy, repair broken relationships, or live a perfect life from that point on. Because our loved one has already died, bargaining with God seems futile. With the death of both children, my bargaining came in the form of "Now you've taken two of my children, and I will live with that, but only if you promise not to take any more of them."

Some bargaining occurred before my babies were born. Subconsciously, I felt there might be a problem with Ammon's arrival. I realized this afterward as I thought about the many worries I'd had that something would go wrong, almost as if they were hints toward the future. The same thing occurred during Kija's pregnancy, except then I was very conscious of it. In both cases, I bargained with God, promising Him that I would be a perfect mother to my new baby, that I would provide all the love he or she deserved, if only He would not take my precious child from me.

Infertile couples grieving for the baby they cannot have may remain in this stage of their grief process for a long time. They may continue to promise Heavenly Father that if He will give them a child, they will devote their lives to Him, never speak a harsh word, and never make a single mistake.

Bargaining often comes with all of the "what ifs" and "if onlys," and can be laden with guilt and regret. I felt an immense amount of guilt throughout every stage of my grieving and was still asking the "what ifs" long after I thought I'd achieved acceptance. Several months after Ammon was born, I was still lying awake at night asking the "what ifs." Had I killed my baby? Could he somehow have recovered if we hadn't given up on him? These doubts about Ammon didn't subside until I called the hospital and talked to the nurse who reassured me that we had made the right decision.

In Kija's situation, even while the doctor was performing the ultrasound, I immediately asked him, "Is it because I've been running?" Had I somehow killed my daughter while running every morning? He assured me that exercise was a good thing and couldn't have been the cause of her death, but I still wondered. I had even run a race during my pregnancy! Even if that hadn't been the cause of her death, surely other people would speculate that it was. I felt guilty and selfish and wished I could turn back time and just vegetate on the couch instead of being physically active. What if I hadn't exercised? Would the outcome have been different? I felt some resolution when I learned that my baby had actually died a week before I ran the race, giving me some solace, but I still asked, "What if?"

I also felt guilty that I had been keeping my pregnancy a secret. What if I had made her feel more welcome by joyously announcing her impending arrival and expressing my excitement outwardly?

A couple of days after returning from Kija's delivery, I received a phone call from my doctor's office. The results of my blood tests were in. Before delivery, the head resident had asked me if there had been any unusual events in the preceding weeks. I told her of a rash that had spread throughout our family and then disappeared. She decided to test me for parvovirus B19, which can harm or even kill unborn babies during the first half of pregnancy. My test results showed that I didn't have the virus at the time of Kija's birth, but that I'd had it sometime in the past. There was no way to know if I'd had it in my early childhood or during my pregnancy. Suddenly I felt an immense amount of guilt—why hadn't I gone to the doctor while I had the rash? Could he have saved Kija's life? And then there were the other pregnant women that my children had come into contact with—what if they had exposed them to this virus and caused harm to their babies as well? I started calling every expectant mother I could think of who had been near my children during the past few weeks and begged them to call their doctors. Thankfully, all of them delivered healthy babies. We will never know whether this mysterious rash had anything to do with Kija's death—her autopsy left us no clues as to the cause. So we were just left to wonder.

I realized that all of my guilty feelings were unfounded and irrational. However, as I said before, grieving mothers are not thinking or feeling rationally. They may outwardly appear to be, but inside they are still battling the "what ifs": What if I had made her feel more welcome? What if I had taken better care of myself? What if I had quit my job or taken more time off? What if I hadn't taken that trip? What if I'd gone to the doctor sooner? If only I could go back and try things differently, maybe I would have received a different outcome. Maybe my baby would still be here. If only God would give me one more chance, I'd do better next time.

As you watch loved ones grieve, it's essential not to blame them for what has happened or how they are acting. They are already blaming themselves enough for both of you. Reassure them that this isn't their fault. Reassure them that they did everything they possibly could have to care for their baby. And most of all, love them unconditionally.

SEVEN
More Than Baby Blues

"O then, if I have seen so great things, if the Lord
in his condescension unto the children of men hath
visited men in so much mercy, why should my
heart weep and my soul linger in the valley of
sorrow, and my flesh waste away, and my strength
slacken, because of mine afflictions?"
—2 Nephi 4:26

A FEW DAYS AFTER KIJA'S delivery, I wrote the following in my journal:

> Yesterday the "baby blues" came, right on schedule,
> so I'm trying to keep busy and am waiting for that
> to pass. It is different from grieving for the baby
> because it's just like there's a dark cloud over every-
> thing. I remember when it came with Rebecca, I
> felt so guilty because here I had this beautiful little
> baby girl who I had waited for for so long and yet I
> felt so sad! Anyway, I'm hoping that it only lasts a
> couple of days and then goes away.

A grieving mother has a doubly hard time with the fourth
stage of grief, depression, because she may also have to deal with
the baby blues, which strike most new mothers to some degree.

I have always been very blessed to have a relatively short
bout with the baby blues, with them usually lasting just a

couple of days. With each of my children it appeared around the third or fourth day after birth. I would cry for no reason and, as I wrote in my journal, I simply felt that a gloomy cloud was resting over me. I would wonder what I had to look forward to now that my baby was already born, and I would feel overwhelmed with the thought of raising this child for eighteen years! When the baby blues passed, I would feel a great sense of relief. Even while mourning the babies I lost, I felt the relief from the baby blues passing. While I didn't feel happy, I could deal with my grief much more easily without the moodiness and low spirits that encompassed me while my hormones were settling.

Often the arrival of baby blues will coincide with a mother's milk coming in, and that's how the timing always worked for me. When you have lost a baby, having your milk come in is just a painful (physically and emotionally) reminder of what you have lost.

My aunt, Patricia Webb, wrote a poem entitled "Why?" that clearly depicts this heart-wrenching feeling:

> Why, Lord?
> Out of all the hundreds, thousands—even
>   millions of babies born each day—
> Why did mine have to be called back to Thee
> Without my ever having known him
> Without my ever having placed his tiny lips
>   upon my breast
> Or feeling his tiny hand curled tightly 'round
>   my finger
> As I gazed into bright, searching eyes?

While our heart aches, so do our breasts, which were given us specifically to feed a baby. When the baby is no longer there, the physical pain makes the emotional pain of the loss much worse.

As I went through the depression stage with the loss of my babies, some days were better than others. Some days were happier than others. Some days I felt at peace and others I felt as if my world was falling apart all around me. I am grateful for those days and even moments of reprieve that helped me to get through the especially dark and desperate times.

As in the case of a baby lost long before its due date, depression may hit again when the due date comes around, reminding the mother of her loss. Ammon was born at thirty-four weeks and was close enough to his due date that I was still dealing with my initial grief and didn't notice much of a difference when his due date approached. With Kija, however, who was born at five months, I was just starting to act "normal" to those around me, and was participating once again in the activities that had kept me busy before, when suddenly I fell back into a deep sadness again—coinciding with her due date. This also happened to be around the time when the baby boom was exploding in my town—babies were being born every week, it seemed. One moment I would feel like I was handling things well, and then I would see a picture of a baby or hear mention of another birth, and I would fall apart.

Quite often it will appear that the depression has come to an end, only to be contradicted with harsh reminders that it is still there, lingering on. The very best advice I can give a woman in this situation is to cry. Climb into bed, pull the covers over your head, and just cry. If your children catch you during your moment of emotion, pull them into your arms and cry with them. Holding it in will exhaust you, and eventually the tears will come anyway—perhaps in a social situation where you would rather appear strong and would be embarrassed for others to see you when you're not.

Being a task-oriented person, I would rarely just sit on the couch and do nothing. I liked to be involved with my kids' activities, working on a project, or expanding my mind in some way. But as I mourned for Kija, there were some days when I did just sit on the couch and watch the kids run back and forth through the living room. I didn't have the desire to get up and play with them or vacuum the floor. I just wanted to sit. Allow yourself this time to rest. There will still be plenty of things to do tomorrow.

If you're on the other side of this situation and feel that your grieving loved one has been depressed for too long, be patient. Everyone grieves at their own pace. Pushing them to "get over it" or trying to convince them that other people's problems are far worse than theirs may cause them to resent you. As long as you are not concerned for their safety or ability to function, allow them as much time as they need to grieve. It will not last forever. Be patient with them. Love them. Cry with them. If you are concerned for your loved one's safety or if they seem unable to function, it would be appropriate for you to encourage them to seek professional help or to seek that help for them. The depression stage of grief is natural, but it can be confused with the serious disease that requires professional help and treatment.

EIGHT

And So Life Goes On

"Now, concerning the state of the soul between death and the resurrection—Behold, it has been made known unto me by an angel, that the spirits of all men, as soon as they are departed from this mortal body, yea, the spirits of all men, whether they be good or evil, are taken home to that God who gave them life. And then shall it come to pass, that the spirits of those who are righteous are received into a state of happiness, which is called paradise, a state of rest, a state of peace, where they shall rest from all their troubles and from all care, and sorrow."

—Alma 40:11–12

THE STAGES OF GRIEF ALL made sense on paper when I learned about them in my college courses. But as I grieved for my babies in real life, I thought there must be something wrong with me because I didn't feel like I was reaching the acceptance stage. To me, acceptance meant that you were all right with what had happened, that you were even happy with how things had come to pass. I never felt that way. I still don't feel that way. I still wish I could go back and do things differently, change things somehow, and have both of my babies back.

It was only recently that I realized I was viewing acceptance in completely the wrong way. Kübler-Ross and Kessler put it perfectly: "Acceptance is often confused with the notion of being all right or okay with what has happened. This is not the case. Most people don't ever feel okay or all right about the loss of a loved one. This stage is about accepting the reality that our loved one is physically gone and recognizing that this new reality is the permanent reality. We will never like this reality or make it okay, but eventually we accept it" (*On Grief and Grieving*, 25).

Acceptance simply means that you decide to go on with life and figure out how to live with your loss. In my case, acceptance slowly came when I realized that the trial of losing Ammon was not meaningless, and many blessings came out of that trial. Even though I didn't like being without him, I knew Heavenly Father still had a plan for him and for our family. Because Ammon was not with us here on earth, we were blessed to have our twins come into our family.

With Kija, finding acceptance was more difficult. While intellectually I knew that sometimes these things just happen, as I'd heard many times, I also felt that so many things had happened in my life for a purpose and surely this couldn't be an exception. It wasn't until after the birth of my last child that I visited a second hematologist who was able to diagnose my blood disorder. Knowing the reason behind my uncontrollable bleeding gave me an added perspective into Kija's loss. If I had carried Kija to full term and received a hysterectomy after her birth as we'd planned, I almost certainly would have bled to death because the doctors wouldn't have known how to treat my undiagnosed blood disorder. Realizing this brought me both peaceful understanding and an intense feeling of guilt—why had my life been spared when Kija's hadn't? What if Heavenly Father could have brought her safely to earth and allowed me to die instead? Eventually, I came to terms with the fact that there are many things that happen to us in life that we will never understand. Someday we will see how all of the puzzle pieces fit together in our lives. Then we will truly appreciate Heavenly Father's great wisdom and love for His children.

Acceptance finally did come. I never would have chosen to go through all the pain, but I did go through it, and when it was finally over, I knew that I would continue to live and to have happiness in life, mixed with sorrow.

Our belief in the gospel and eternal families may help bring acceptance sooner. It may be easier to accept the death of a loved one when we know that we will be with them for eternity. But in some ways I think our knowledge of the gospel also makes grieving harder. It did for me, anyway, because we believe in a loving Father in Heaven who will grant blessings according to our obedience. If we pay our tithing, He will open the windows of heaven that there will not be room enough to receive the blessings. If we honor our father and mother, our days will be lengthened upon the earth. As I grieved for Kija, I was teaching the Primary children in our ward about the many promises that Heavenly Father makes to us in the scriptures based upon our obedience. I thought that surely having a child should have been similar to these other commandments, with a promise of a healthy, living baby attached as a reward for obedience to the commandment to raise righteous families. It may be harder to come to peace with the death of a loved one when we know that we have tried our best to choose the right and to be a good person. To a grieving Latter-day Saint mother, this makes no sense. Yet, our faith in Heavenly Father's plan and His love for us eventually persuade us to accept the reality of our lives—we are blessed for our righteousness, but we also need to be tried and tested. Things may not happen the way we hope, but life will go on, and we can allow ourselves to feel joy again.

Sometimes I think acceptance is mistaken for peace. I think that a person can feel peace eventually, but acceptance comes much sooner. Slowly, as the days, weeks, months, and even years pass, we will realize that we do feel peace.

Soon after Ammon's death I wrote these thoughts in my journal:

I have thought of so many "if onlys" and "what ifs." I lie awake at night crying and agonizing over them. But it always ends in the same way: it was supposed to happen this way just simply because it *did* happen this way. If it were supposed to happen any other way, Heavenly Father would have notified me with flashing lights before my eyes: GET TO THE HOSPITAL NOW!!! But He didn't. Even though I unconsciously knew something was wrong all along and felt something like this was going to happen, I never felt any prompting to do anything about it at all—until I called the hospital that night. And every time I think about that I am amazed by the miracle of it. And so, while I may have been tempted to be mad at Heavenly Father for taking my son, instead I am overwhelmed and extremely grateful that He cared enough to allow me two days to spend with my son.

NINE

A *Child's* Sorrow

"Behold, ye are little children and ye cannot bear all things now; ye must grow in grace and in the knowledge of the truth. Fear not, little children, for you are mine, and I have overcome the world, and you are of them that my Father hath given me; And none of them that my Father hath given me shall be lost."

—D&C 50:40–42

IN MANY WAYS, THE LOSS of my brother shaped my view of life. I knew that bad things could happen to good people, but I also believed that sadness should be balanced out with happiness. After accepting his loss, I decided that I should never again have to feel so much sorrow. I felt that I deserved only joy after already receiving my share of heartache.

My parents provided a valuable gift to me by allowing me to grieve and by allowing me to see them grieve. I learned that it was okay to cry. It was okay to talk about Cory. It was even okay to be angry about what had happened.

More than twenty years later, when Kija died while yet inside of me, I watched the reactions of each of my children. Cameron, age ten, and Micah, age nine, reacted in much the same way I had upon learning that my brother Cory had died. Cameron was very concerned for my welfare. He worried and fretted, calling me quite often at the hospital to make sure I was all right. But when he visited me, he joked around and tried to lighten the mood, as if not wanting to show that he was hurting. We worried about whether he might not really be dealing with the situation. In fact, we asked the hospital social worker to meet with him because we were so worried about his joking and light behavior. We realized that he was probably in denial, and we hoped that talking to her—a neutral person not currently experiencing grief—would help him work through his feelings.

Several months after Kija's death, I asked Cameron how he had felt about the experience. With sudden tears in his eyes he said that it made him sad to see me so sad, and that he felt gloomy for a long time, "Sort of like an itch that never goes away." Cameron had a schoolteacher who lost a baby at the same time we did. I noticed that he spoke with her often about the experience, as if he were grateful to have someone outside the family to discuss it with. Also knowing that our experience was not an isolated one seemed to make it feel more "normal" to him and thus easier to deal with. I was grateful for her willingness to talk with Cameron, despite her own grief. I think he felt that if he talked to me about it, it would make me sad so he tried to bring it up as little as possible. If I initiated the conversation, however, Cameron was very willing and anxious to talk.

I think that both age and birth order affected Cameron's reaction to Kija's death. Because he is the oldest child, as I was, he felt a need to protect his younger siblings and even his parents. Years after Ammon's death, when we were discussing the decisions we had to make, while his younger siblings asked questions like, "How big was the life support machine?" Cameron asked, "What did that feel like?" He wanted to understand our emotions.

Because all of our children had been in the room during the ultrasound that revealed our baby's lifeless body, nine-year-old Micah asked me afterward, "Mom, next time you're going to have a baby, will you go to the doctor and make sure it's alive before you tell us about it?" Micah didn't seem to feel the need to discuss his grief as much as Cameron did. He also didn't put on a happy facade, making us worry that he wasn't handling it well or that he was still in denial. When I asked him about it, though, he admitted to me that he did cry about it when no one was watching. He felt the same need I did to grieve privately. He told me months afterward that he was still sad about Kija's death—that, in fact, he was still sad about Ammon dying. He was only a toddler when Ammon died, but the association he had with his other siblings made him realize what he was missing with Ammon. Micah was often the first to bring up Ammon when people were discussing our family. When people asked about the ages of our children, Micah would routinely add, "And Ammon would be seven if he were here." Sometimes when setting the table, he placed an extra table setting. When I asked what it was for, he matter-of-factly said, "Ammon." It seemed that Micah had decided it was his responsibility to make sure no one forgot about Ammon or Kija.

Ethan and Ian, the seven-year-old twins, told us of their sadness but then quickly went on with their lives while still mentioning Kija often. Jamey, age six, had been especially excited about the upcoming arrival of Kija and had made his own preparations for her, arranging blankets and his stuffed animals in the cradle. When we announced our next pregnancy, Jamey immediately began praying very fervently for the baby in very specific terms—"Please don't let the baby die after it comes out of Mom's tummy like Ammon did, and please don't let the baby die before it comes out of Mom's tummy like Kija did. Please make the baby be alive." I didn't see any of these three shed any tears over the loss, and usually their mention of Ammon or Kija would be in a very matter-of-fact way. They often brought it up at social gatherings, quite often in a way that was very embarrassing for me because it was not something I wanted to talk about right then. All three often told strangers about Ammon and Kija, leaving the stranger to wonder how they ought to react. It almost seemed that they viewed it as a unique show-and-tell topic because none of their friends had ever lost a sibling. They wanted to know details about the equipment, the events, and the facts. Sometimes it seemed that they asked the same questions over and over again.

Teancum, age four, was obsessed with "bringing the babies back to life." He talked about this often for several weeks after we buried Kija. When we visited their graves at the cemetery, he ran from grave to grave talking about each "baby" that was buried there. It didn't occur to him that people of all ages die. His only experiences with death involved babies—his older brother Ammon, whom we talked about frequently, and his younger sister Kija, whose loss he had experienced. When I became pregnant with our tenth child, Teancum asked very matter-of-factly, "Is this going to be a graveyard baby or a take-home baby?" He joined Jamey in praying that our baby would not die. Even after our youngest, Elizabeth, was born, Teancum continued to pray at night, in family prayer, and in blessings on the food, "Please don't let Elizabeth die like Ammon did."

Rebecca, age two, was unaware of most of what was going on. She knew that there had been a "baby in my tummy," but having never experienced a baby in the house, she didn't realize that anything was missing. Similar to how Cameron and Micah had acted when Ammon died, Rebecca was mostly oblivious to what the family was going through. When Rebecca reached preschool age, however, she started to ask numerous questions about both Ammon and Kija. Most of her questions centered around their physical appearance—such as their hair color or size—but some of her other questions revealed the worries she was starting to have about her own mortality. Why did Ammon and Kija die when they were babies instead of when they were old? Were they sick? Why didn't they get better? Am I going to die too?

I didn't realize it as a nine-year-old, but my experience with the death of my brother helped to shape my opinions, my interactions with people, and my perception of motherhood. Logically, it made sense that children of all ages would react to death in different ways because each of them is so developmentally different. Still, it surprised me how vastly different my children's reactions were to Kija's death. It reinforced the importance of helping each child deal with death and grief on an individual level.

The most important thing I did for my children was to accept the way they chose to grieve. Parents have a natural desire to protect or shield their children from pain, but I knew this would not help my children in the long run. I knew they needed to grieve just as I needed to grieve. I also realized that each of them would be different, and that I needed to embrace those differences rather than persuade my children to behave the way I thought they ought to.

In an experience of loss, it might bother you that your children aren't acting as sad as you think they should. I discovered that some of my children did not need to cry, and that was okay. Some of my other children did need to cry, and that was okay too. The generalization that boys don't cry has to be overlooked because boys, just like girls, need to grieve. If I tried to prevent them from expressing their emotions, they were sure to experience the same physical problems that I would experience if I didn't cry. My advice is to let your children cry. Cry with them. Allow them to see you cry. They are watching you for cues as to how they should be behaving. If they never see your sadness, they may think that there must be something wrong with them because they feel so sad.

I also recommend allowing children to express their anger. They experience the stages of grief also, and anger is one of those stages. Some of my children threw tantrums or had other angry outbursts, even though I thought they should be too old for such things. But I realized that my children had probably never had any greater reason to be angry than they did over the death of a sibling. They weren't sure how to express the great amount of anger they felt inside. While you shouldn't condone unacceptable behavior such as harming another person, patiently helping your children to express their anger may help them to move on. I encouraged my older children to write their feelings in their journals. When they spoke to me about their angry feelings, I did not reprimand them or tell them that they shouldn't feel this way. The truth was that they *did* feel this way, and nothing I could say was going to change that. Allowing them to feel angry was a necessary step in their healing.

Some children may regress soon after the death of their sibling. My four-year-old son Teancum started having nightmares and wetting the bed, even though he'd been potty trained for some time. Showing alarm at your child's regressing behavior might make it worse. In Teancum's case, not reprimanding the bed-wetting and comforting him after his nightmares proved to be the solution to the problem. He soon started sleeping through the night and staying dry again.

Children are naturally curious, so one important thing I did for my children was to allow them to ask the many questions they had, and to answer them as honestly as possible. Even months and years after the loss of their siblings, my children were still asking questions. "What did Ammon look like?" "Why did he die?" "Why didn't the doctors fix him?" "If he were alive now, do you think he would look like me?" "Why couldn't we see Kija?" "What did she look like?" "What color eyes did she have?" "How big was she?" All of my children asked questions, and we answered all of them to the best of our abilities. As an adult, I sometimes still ask my mom questions about her experiences surrounding Cory's death. I want to understand, and I realize that my children have that same yearning to understand. They are figuring out so many things about life, and death is part of life. It may be painful for some mothers to talk about the details of their baby's death, but I think it is important to be as open and honest as possible.

If talking with a child about the death of a baby is too painful for the mother, she can encourage the child to talk to a grandparent or counselor who is willing to answer questions and listen to his or her feelings without being judgmental or emotionally reactive.

Children are very resilient. Even though we want to protect them from experiencing the pain, we must realize that they will eventually heal. We can comfort each other along the way.

TEN

How Can I Help?

". . . Yea, and are willing to mourn with those that mourn; yea, and comfort those that stand in need of comfort, and to stand as witnesses of God at all times and in all things, and in all places that ye may be in, even until death, that ye may be redeemed of God, and be numbered with those of the first resurrection, that ye may have eternal life—"
—Mosiah 18:9

AS A GRIEVING MOTHER, I realized that many people around me were also hurting. I knew that my family members and friends loved me. They were grieving for the loss of my baby and were also grieving for the pain they knew I was feeling. My mother and mother-in-law had each experienced the loss of babies, and they were hurting for their lost grandchild, for their hurting daughter and son, and for their own lost children—an experience they both remembered all too clearly after so many years. I knew they wished they could make it all better, as did the other people around me.

Parents will handle their grief in a variety of ways. Some of them want a shoulder to cry on, while others prefer to cry into their pillow. Some want someone to talk to and keep them company, while others want to grieve privately. I was the latter. I preferred to be left alone for several reasons. One was simply the practical fact that I look horrible when I cry. My face gets all blotchy, red, and puffy, and my eyes nearly swell shut. I didn't want anyone to see me looking like that. Another reason was that I didn't want to feel like I had to keep the house clean because people would be dropping by at any minute to visit and comfort me. Rationally, I knew that no one would mind a few toys out on the floor, but as we know, grieving people are not always thinking logically.

Another reason for my isolation after Kija passed was the abundance of unintentionally hurtful comments that I received after Ammon's passing. I thought that if I avoided people, they would not be given the opportunity to say anything that would hurt me. I didn't want to have to retell the story innumerable times, reliving it over and over again, or have to answer a myriad of questions that well-meaning people might ask me. I also just plain wanted to be alone. *On Grief and Grieving* states, "Feeling isolated after loss is normal, expected, and healthy. Even when friends urge you to talk about it (they are certainly being caring), you wonder what there is to say. Sometimes people's desire to deliver you from your isolation may have more to do with their own fear and discomfort than with a concern for yours" (81). Forcing a person to return to normal life or resume normal activities before they are ready may cause them to resent you later.

After I lost my babies, I didn't want to do any of the things that I had done before, or be around any of the people I had spent time with before because I feared it would remind me of my pregnancy, or of the days when I used to be happy—days that were gone now. Some of my friends were hurt that I wanted to isolate myself, but I didn't have the energy to meet both their needs and mine, so I just waited patiently for them to understand.

If a person asks to be left alone, it is best to respect their desires. This does not mean, however, that you forget about or ignore them. A kind note, card, or e-mail would be appreciated greatly. I saved every card, note, and e-mail that I received after Ammon's and Kija's passings and placed them in scrapbooks I made for them. It meant a great deal to me that people cared, and that they reached out to me in this way. Mail is delivered in such a nonthreatening way that even those who want to stay isolated can handle the contact. I never worried about whether the postman thought my hair was unkempt; I would go out and get the mail anyway. Even if your grieving friend or family member is not in self-imposed isolation, a note or card is always a lasting reminder of how much you care.

Be careful what you say. Grieving people are often more sensitive than they would otherwise be. Many people said things to or around me that hurt greatly, and yet they certainly had no malicious intentions. I quickly learned that people who had not been through a similar event in their lives truly had no idea how much what they said might hurt. After losing Ammon, I thought back on the many insensitive things I had done and said to grieving women over the years, and I felt horrible. I even approached some of them and apologized. I had no idea that the little things I said or did might bring them additional heartache.

So, being limited in what to say to a grieving mother, should you just remain silent? Maybe. You can always say, "I love you," or, "I care about you." But a silent hug given through tears can also speak a million loving words. Even just honestly saying, "I don't know what to say" can be helpful, because they still know you care. "Think before you speak" is some very good advice during this sensitive time. If you don't know what to say to your friend, try writing your feelings in a note. Don't, however, pretend that nothing has happened when you see your grieving friend. She may not want to talk about her experience, but she also doesn't want to be ignored or avoided.

Sometimes, admittedly, there is just no avoiding hurting a grieving person with your words or actions, because they are going to grieve despite them, and at the time that you are trying to comfort your grieving friend, they may be in the anger stage of their grieving process. Even one misspoken word can be like a dagger to the heart, and it then becomes the grieving mother's responsibility to eventually reconcile her hurt feelings and realize that the innocent bystanders had no ill intent. Even after losing two children, I don't always know what to say to a grieving mother. People are so individual, and the words that will help or hurt them will be so different. There is not one magic phrase that will deliver your feelings of love, caring, and comfort. Nothing you can say will bring her baby back and, in her mind, right now that may be the only acceptable solution.

There are, however, some phrases to avoid. I don't think it is ever comforting to start a sentence with "At least" or "You're lucky because . . ." A grieving mother is *not* lucky. And saying "at least" may seem to her that you are diminishing the greatness of her loss. "At least you got to hold your baby." "At least you had some time with your baby." "At least you can still have more children." "At least you have other children at home." "At least you have the gospel." I heard that statement so many times that I even heard myself saying it to another grieving mother before I caught myself and thought, *How could I say that?* Yes, we have the gospel, but that certainly doesn't make it any easier to live without our beloved baby *right now.* Our baby is still not *with us* where we think he or she *should* be.

The mistake commonly made around me was to compare my loss to other, much greater losses. "I know a woman who lost five babies . . ." or, "In my day you didn't even get to see your baby if it died before it was born." These statements may all be true, but a grieving mother is deservedly selfish and is not thinking about the grief that others have gone through in the past. She is buried in her own grief, and that is what she needs to concentrate on. She is fully aware that other people have been through much harder trials than hers, but at that moment in her life, only the Savior could really say that He'd been through more pain than she is currently experiencing. While your intention is to comfort her, she may feel that you are attempting to minimize her pain, and that is not what she needs. She needs validation of her grief.

I discovered that the exception to this rule was with some of the women who had previously lost babies themselves. Somehow they knew not to try to make their loss seem greater than mine, and yet they brought me comfort in knowing that they had made it through their own grief. So many women who I hadn't known had lost babies suddenly came out of the woodwork. Even women whom I barely knew were approaching me, telling me the most personal events of their lives and crying as they spoke. It is one of the biggest "clubs" on earth, in which none of the members want to be invited—the Grieving Mothers Club, you could call it. It will always exist, and its members will always long to provide support to new members—perhaps because it brings normalcy to their own experience, or perhaps because they simply want to alleviate some of the suffering they know this mother is going through. I discovered that especially older women who had lost babies longed to talk to me about it. Because the subject of the birth experience was not often discussed in the past, I suspected that they had not been able to openly talk about the experiences surrounding their losses. Even after all of these years they had the desire to share their most deeply held feelings. They remember.

Another important thing to avoid is to in any way blame the mother for what has happened. I went to console a friend who had lost a baby soon into her second trimester, and her husband told me that he feared the baby's death was caused by his wife moving furniture around the day before. I wondered why on earth he would say that. While it may be a valid concern, how could that help? Losing a baby is very rarely a mother's fault, and saying things like, "I wish you had eaten more" or, "I wish you had rested more" only enforces the doubts and guilt she is already experiencing. This is not helpful. On the contrary, a grieving mother needs reassurance that this is *not* her fault, that she did everything possible to care for her baby, and that there was nothing more she could have done. Imagine the guilt she would live with for the rest of her life if she went on thinking she had somehow caused her baby's death!

When my husband called our bishop from the Denver hospital to tell him what had happened, I overheard the bishop ask, "Is it because she traveled?" While at first I felt resentment for being blamed for Ammon's situation, I quickly realized that he might have been asking out of his own feelings of guilt, because if he hadn't made arrangements to interview me for my temple recommend, I would not have gone to Denver in the first place. I later reassured him that I considered his special efforts on my behalf to be a priceless gift that afforded me a chance to spend two days with my living son. I suspect that my friend's husband was also reacting out of his own guilt, wishing that he had been the one moving furniture instead of his wife.

It is also important that you do not judge how a woman is grieving. Never say, "You've been angry long enough, it's time to move on" or, "Will you be depressed forever?" Grieving mothers need your acceptance and love, not your advice and judgment. Behaving in this way may permanently damage your relationship, even long after they have reached acceptance. Be patient. Every mother will move through the grief process at her own speed. She will reach one stage and sometimes return to another. This is normal and healthy, and she needs your support throughout the experience. If you feel that because of her isolation she is neglecting you and your friendship, try very hard to respect her feelings to be alone. As long as you are not worried about her safety, let her grieve at her own pace.

If you are an expectant mother or have a new baby, don't be surprised if your grieving friend avoids you. Seeing your growing belly or your healthy, chubby baby is only a painful reminder of what she has lost. In Sherri Wittwer's book *Gone Too Soon,* she shares the feelings of a grieving mother who said, "I know it's irrational, but I felt as if Heavenly Father took my baby away and gave it to my friend" (31). This is very similar to how I felt with both Ammon and Kija. As I've shared, five of my six sisters-in-law all had healthy babies shortly after Ammon died, and there was the baby boom in my community soon after Kija died. When I looked at these babies, I didn't think, "That is my baby. Heavenly Father took it away and gave it to her." But I *did* think, "That should be me holding that baby and feeling that happiness." As I've watched my nieces grow up over these past many years, I have often thought of the similar stages that Ammon would be going through at their various milestones. A grieving mother usually remembers the age that her baby would be had he or she been alive. She is probably very aware of the children who are close to her baby's age. This can be painful, at times, to watch them grow and have a happy, healthy life. She not only grieves her baby's death; she also grieves each milestone that he or she is missing out on.

After Kija died, I found myself not only avoiding pregnant women or new mothers, but also any woman of childbearing age. Just knowing that they could have something that I did not have was too much for me to bear. Several months later one of my friends called me. She told me that she'd had a dream in which I wrapped my arms around her and told her, "I love you, but it hurts me so much to see your baby." She tearfully told me of her love for me and apologized for any pain that it caused me to be around her or her baby. I explained that it had been very hard to be around not only hers, but all of the new babies that were being born in our small town, and that I truly appreciated her phone call. She asked if it might help if I "borrowed" her baby for a couple of hours. I kindly told her that this would probably be too hard for me.

I thought of the similar comment the woman made to my mother when I was nine years old and was so grateful that my friend had asked me over the phone rather than while standing over me with her baby—a situation that may have made me feel obligated to hold her baby in order to spare her own hurt feelings. I was truly grateful for my friend's honesty with me about her feelings. She had been feeling neglected by me because we had been very close before. She was sad that I hadn't been more excited to see or want to hold her baby, and this perhaps led to a dream that gave her more understanding of how I felt. Asking (from a distance) if it would help to hold your baby, rather than just dropping your baby in a grieving mother's arms, is a good idea. There are some grieving women who long to hold a baby—whose arms ache for one—and holding your baby may provide them a great deal of comfort. The key is to not impose your own feelings upon them. Perhaps you think holding someone else's baby would be helpful to you while grieving, but it might just be heartbreaking to your friend. If the announcement to her of your pregnancy can be delayed while your friend grieves a little longer, she will be very grateful later. It isn't that she doesn't love you and that she can't be genuinely happy for you later, but right now it is a very painful reminder of what she has lost.

Something to keep in mind is that while a mother is grieving, she is probably not taking the best care of her body. Diet and exercise are often placed on the back burner. She may still appear to be pregnant even several months after her baby is born.

Perhaps in part because of this, rumors were spreading throughout my ward soon after I lost Ammon that I was pregnant again, long before I actually was. I was anxious myself to get pregnant again, but my plans did not fall into place quite the way I had hoped. With rumors swirling around the ward that I was pregnant again, I felt even more pain as I waited to conceive. I desperately wished to be pregnant once more, and having people assume that I was made the reality that I was not harder to bear. People were approaching me saying, "I heard you're pregnant again! Congratulations!" I finally asked the Relief Society president to put an end to such rumors and gently tell the Relief Society sisters that I was not pregnant again. I knew of their love for me and their hope that I would feel happiness again. Their joy over thinking I was pregnant was genuine, and they were disappointed along with me when they discovered that I was not.

A great misconception, however, is that when a grieving mother gets pregnant again, suddenly she is "all better." This is not the case. Grieving continues. Just as you love each of your children individually, you still grieve for the one you lost even though you have another one on the way. The relief I felt with being able to conceive another baby was that this pregnancy would keep my mind occupied, would give me something to look forward to, and reassured me that I had at least one more chance at motherhood. Some grieving mothers are never able to conceive again. As one mother who lost her last baby more than ten years ago told me, "You never recover from that." Whether another baby follows or not, a mother will grieve at various times for the rest of her life for the baby that she lost. Something will remind her of her pain, and she'll suddenly start to cry, even years later. Just as motherhood is a lifelong commitment, grieving for a lost child is a lifelong process. When I lost my two babies, my mother grieved yet again for the baby she'd lost many years earlier.

So, you're wondering, what on earth can I do? It seems like a no-win situation! Yes, it may seem so, but don't give up. Don't abandon your grieving loved one just because you're not sure what to do. If she wants to be alone, let her know you will be available as soon as she's ready. Send a note. Drop off a meal. Mow her lawn.

Sending flowers is a good idea. Often a mother who is burying her baby cannot stand the thought of leaving his or her grave bare. If you are purchasing flowers specifically for the baby's grave, be sure they have a wide base so they won't be easily knocked over. If they are living flowers, be sure they will be able to withstand the current weather conditions. If they are silk flowers, be sure the base is heavy enough that they will not blow away. A floral spray is also nice, but if the casket is tiny, as in the case of our Kija, you may not be able to see it under a large spray. Consider the circumstances, and if you suspect that your loved one may not have flowers to leave on her baby's grave or to keep in her home, bring some to her or have them delivered. They will be greatly appreciated.

While some women want to remain silent, some women really feel the need to talk. I realized this over the years as many grieving mothers wanted to tell me their stories. Some of them had a need to tell their stories over and over again, even though the story ended the same way every time. While I was one who preferred not to repeat my story, writing it in this book has been therapeutic for me, almost as if a resolution has been reached simply by putting the words onto paper. If your grieving friend doesn't feel like talking out loud, perhaps she would greatly welcome a journal to write her thoughts in. Her words would then be safe from judgment by those who might not understand her.

Sometimes when you don't know what to say, a book can say it for you. After the loss of my babies, I received books as bereavement gifts. I read all of them cover to cover. For someone who doesn't normally enjoy reading, it seemed that I was thirsting for any comfort or direction I could find. I wanted to feel normal. I wanted to know that I was not alone.

A few of the gifts that were especially meaningful to me were little objects that represented my babies. After Ammon died, I received two figurines that I put in a special place where I could keep remembrances of him. After Kija died, one of my good friends gave me a bracelet inscribed to read, REMEMBER, and had Kija's birthstone set in it. This was such a meaningful gift that I would never have thought of, but one that I treasured. One of our friends gave us a small yellow rosebush in remembrance of Ammon. I planted it in our front yard and thought of him each time I passed it. Years after we had moved from our home in Moab, I went back on a vacation and drove past our old house. I smiled as I saw that Ammon's beautiful rosebush was still there—a wonderful reminder of the love we have for him.

There are myriad acts of service that you can perform on behalf of a grieving friend. When I was in the hospital in Denver, my visiting teaching partner called and offered to drive six hours to pick up my boys and bring them home and take care of them until I returned. I am still greatly touched by that offer of help. Caring for the surviving children of a grieving mother is a great act of service. Even taking them to the park so that she can have one quiet afternoon will provide her a chance to be alone with her thoughts and perhaps get some needed rest. Don't be pushy, however. While I appreciated my mother caring for Cameron and Micah after Ammon's death, after Kija's death I only wanted my children around me, and it would have thrown me deeper into sadness had someone come and taken them from me. As always, it is important to respect a grieving mother's wishes.

Something that I was not able to handle at the time of Ammon's death was planning all the funeral details. We had never expected the death of a child, so we didn't have burial plots. We'd never shopped around for caskets. We weren't aware of the various fees involved in burying a person. James's mom offered to take care of these details, and I gladly agreed. She went to the funeral home to dress Ammon for burial and discovered that the oils from his body had stained his little white suit. She took the suit home and washed it, then lovingly dressed him for burial. James's parents provided us with a burial plot for Ammon, and later they did the same for Kija. They paid the expenses for his casket and burial fees. We were able to choose any of the important details, such as the color of the casket and the design, color, and style of the headstone, then James's siblings each contributed and paid for Ammon's headstone.

After Kija's death, I was able and wanted to plan her burial details. Because of the generosity of the funeral home owner, we were spared the cost of her tiny casket and the preparation of her body, thus giving us the possibility to have a burial instead of a cremation. Just having the opportunity to decide was such a blessing. My parents and one of my close friends helped to pay for Kija's headstone, which I had chosen and designed to match Ammon's. The bottom of her stone reads, STILL AT BIRTH . . . STILL IN OUR HEARTS. When I look at the two headstones, I think of them as treasured memorials to our babies given to us by our loved ones.

If you are financially able, helping with the funeral or burial costs may be greatly appreciated by a grieving couple. Financial stress on top of the stress of grieving can feel overwhelming at these times. And there are so many financial stresses associated with the death of a baby, whether they be burial expenses, travel expenses, or high medical costs. Even if a couple has life insurance on their children, most policies do not cover stillborn babies. This was the case with Kija. To alleviate some of the costs, we asked the cemetery office if we could dig the hole ourselves. They told us that we could, but we would still be charged the same fee for opening the ground. Such financial stressors can intensify the feelings of grief as a couple realizes that they are paying a great deal of money to bury a baby they will not be able to enjoy.

If a grieving friend is not burying her baby, or not purchasing a headstone, you can make a donation to the college or mission funds of her surviving children in memory of the child she lost. You can also donate money to a charity in the name of the child. Think of what your grieving friend may value, and you will have a good idea what might be a meaningful gift for her.

Many people have asked me if, given a specific situation, they should do something for the grieving person. My advice is always the same: if you know someone well enough to wonder if you ought to do something, then you definitely ought to do something. A heartfelt note can be a comfort to a grieving mother for months and even years afterward. If you feel the need to do something, then *do it.*

How Can I Help?

* a heartfelt note, card, or e-mail
* flowers
* a book
* a rosebush or live plant
* help with tending the surviving children
* help with dishes, laundry, or cleaning the house
* provide meals
* yard work
* a figurine, bracelet, or some other memorial
* financial help with funeral or burial costs
* support or help with burial decisions
* a donation to a charity in the child's name
* a donation to surviving children's mission or college funds
* a shoulder to cry on or a listening ear

ELEVEN
*R*emember Me

"And I am filled with charity, which is everlasting love; wherefore, all children are alike unto me; wherefore, I love little children with a perfect love; and they are all alike and partakers of salvation."
—Moroni 8:17

WHILE THE PAIN FROM THE loss of a baby may be something that a grieving mother wants to forget as soon as possible, her baby is someone she wants to remember. One of the things I'm most grateful for now, following the years since Ammon's passing, is that I had the presence of mind to take the video camera and film my hospital room, Ammon's corner in the NICU, the nurses who were there, the flowers I received, the remembrances that the hospital gave me, and even myself in my hospital gown. While it was a painful process at the time, it brought me comfort months and years later when I could watch it again and remember Ammon's short time on earth.

I created scrapbooks for both Ammon and Kija, including pictures, birth and death certificates, obituaries, hospital wristbands, cards, e-mails, and even some flattened and dried flowers. I created a cross-stitch for Ammon with his name and birthdate on it and put it in the center of a large frame with pictures of him surrounding it. I also created a wreath with many of the flowers that I received when Ammon died. I wrote a poem in his honor and shared it in our family Christmas card. Over the years as we have visited Ammon's and Kija's graves, we have taken pictures of our children there and included them in Ammon's and Kija's scrapbooks. Although Ammon's and Kija's bodies are not growing, our surviving children and family are growing, and we want them to be a part of that. This is the best way we know to accomplish that.

I also kept much of Ammon's hospital paraphernalia, including the blankets he was wrapped in, some of the tubes that were attached to him, and the sheepskin that he had lain on. I keep these in a special place. Every now and then I take them out to look at and remember. A couple of times I have taught a sharing time to the Primary children and brought these special remembrances of Ammon as I talk about eternal families. I even have one of his tiny diapers. Although he never wore it, knowing that it was meant for him made it a keepsake for me.

For Kija I made a memory quilt in which each square represented a different area of her life, including each of her siblings, her brief mortal experience, and her eternal life. The hospital gave me molds of Kija's hands and feet that I keep in my bedroom. I also have hats that belonged to both Kija and Ammon, gifts from the hospital.

For each of my deceased babies I created a birth announcement that I sent to my friends and family, just as I had done for each of my living children. We placed obituaries in the newspaper for both babies. I was searching for ways to add validity to their short lives. Somehow, announcing their births and deaths was an important part of the grief process for me.

For Ammon's eighth birthday, I created a picture slide show set to a lullaby that I mailed to many of my family and friends. It was so important to me that they not forget him. Many people told me they were very touched by it. It provided additional reminders of Ammon's existence here on earth and allowed me to pay tribute to him.

The first anniversary of Ammon's death was a painful one for me. I was pregnant with Jamey, I had twin babies, and two rambunctious toddlers kept me busy. Still, I longed for Ammon in such a painful way. After making it through that first anniversary, my husband and I decided to establish "Ammon Days." Each year on his birthday, we would do something that he would have enjoyed doing if he had been here. We turned his birthday into a celebration. We have shared a variety of activities over the years, ranging from going to Burger King for dinner, to a family boating trip, to a trip to Rapid City, South Dakota. When Kija was born, one day before Ammon's birthday, it seemed only natural that "Ammon Days" would suddenly turn into "Ammon and Kija Days." This was a wonderful way to involve the kids and help them feel like we weren't forgetting their siblings who were no longer with us.

On Ammon's eighth birthday we placed eight white balloons on his grave. The next year this evolved into a tradition of the children releasing balloons on Ammon's and Kija's birthdays. As they release the balloons and watch them float to heaven, the children think of a promise they will make to Ammon and Kija. It is to be something to work on, thus making themselves more worthy to be with their brother and sister again someday.

Having a grave to visit for both Ammon and Kija has brought me so much comfort. Even though I know that only their bodies are there, I feel it is a place I can come and remember them. Women who lose babies early in their pregnancy may not have a plot in the cemetery to visit. Instead, they can plant a tree or devote a special place in their yard or home to this baby they have lost.

On my living room wall hang pictures of each of my children. Ammon and Kija are no exception. We don't have a picture of Kija's body, but in its place we have a picture of our family with her casket at her graveside service. I've received some questioning looks and comments about the picture, hanging amidst my other children's formal school poses, but people soon understand that I feel Kija is still one of my children and I want to remember her and treat her just like the others. Ammon and Kija both have Christmas stockings that we hang on the fireplace with the others. I have discovered that it is as important to my other children as it is to me that Ammon and Kija be remembered. We don't have Ammon and Kija here with us physically, but they are not forgotten by anyone who enters our home.

Conclusion

"Wherefore, children shall grow up until they become old; old men shall die; but they shall not sleep in the dust, but they shall be changed in the twinkling of an eye. Wherefore, for this cause preached the apostles unto the world the resurrection of the dead."

—D&C 63:51–52

WHETHER A MOTHER LOSES A baby two weeks after conception or two weeks after birth, she grieves for it. Kija was not full term, but she still had a body. I believe she still had a spirit, and she was still my baby. I grieved for her as completely as I grieved for Ammon. Sometimes people think that the earlier in pregnancy you lose a baby, the easier it should be to recover from it. My situation taught me that this isn't true. Women I know who have had early miscarriages have explained that they have grieved and felt incredible pain, just as I did. And because grief is such an individual process for everyone, how can we say that a woman who has an early miscarriage doesn't grieve just as deeply as a woman who has a stillborn baby at nine months? Either way they have lost a child—*their* child.

Another myth some people believe is that mothers of several children feel less grief at losing a child than a mother of few children. Someone once told me that because I had several children, I couldn't love them as much as one child that I could give my whole heart to. That was nonsense, of course, because I love each of my children with my whole heart. Having an additional child did not diminish the love I already felt for my other children, or vice versa. Similarly, I learned through experience that grieving for your baby is no less painful when you have several surviving children than it is when you have only one or two. The only difference is that you will be busier when you return home to several children, and you'll have more children who need help and understanding as they also journey through the grief process.

My purpose in writing this book is to let other grieving mothers know that they are normal, they are not alone, and they will make it through the grief process sooner or later. I also wanted to let those around them have a peek into what they are going through, while offering some advice about how to help them while they grieve.

I have made little mention of a father's grief. This was not by accident. I am very aware that fathers grieve just as fully as mothers do, but I could never do it justice to write about it. I will leave that to a grieving father who would like to attempt to put it into words. I know by watching both my husband and father that losing a baby can change a man forever, and his grief is just as real and just as painful as his wife's. My husband went back to work while I grieved at home, and he answered over and over again the question, "How is your wife doing?" Because he was fulfilling his responsibilities and going on with life the way it had been before, others might not have thought to ask, "How are *you* doing?" We buried Kija during his lunch hour. When he returned to work, I doubt anyone knew that he'd just buried his baby. I see men as truly miraculous beings. They tenderly comfort their wives, cry with them, care for them, and then face the world with courage and fortitude.

Although learning about the stages of grief in a social work classroom was different from actually experiencing them in my own life, I was grateful to have been given a formal education that prepared me to deal with the experiences I would later have. It helped me feel normal to realize that the emotions I felt and the stages I went through were similar to what countless others had experienced. As Kübler-Ross and Kessler put it, "Why grieve? For two reasons. First, those who grieve well, live well. Second, and most important, grief is the healing process of the heart, soul, and mind; it is the path that returns us to wholeness. It shouldn't be a matter of *if* you will grieve; the question is *when* you will grieve. And until we do, we suffer from the effects of that unfinished business" (*On Grief and Grieving,* 229). So while the world tells us to "get over it," "be strong," or "go on with life," we owe it to ourselves and to our babies to allow the grief process to take place. We cannot make it go away. We may postpone it, but it will still happen sooner or later.

As you grieve, life will continue to happen. Babies will still be born. People will still go to work. Children will still go to school. And you will grieve. But then, one day, you'll wake up and realize that you went a whole day without crying for your baby. Although you might feel guilty at first, you will quickly realize that you are on the path to acceptance.

Life did not unfold as I had planned. I had my share of sorrow, but I also survived a variety of trials. I had plenty of happiness. I learned many lessons about life, love, and loss. There is no real consolation for a life lived without my two precious babies, but their memory now brings me more joy than pain. While I still shed a tear from time to time, usually I think of them with a smile and look forward to the day when I will once again hold them in my arms. I wonder if they are able to look in on me every now and then and if they yearn to tell me of their love. I feel that as I strive to live righteously I am bringing myself one step at a time closer to being worthy to be with them again, and this motivates and comforts me.

When my babies died, I felt like one of Christ's sheep, lost on a dark and stormy night, and He came searching for me. He did not take the pain away—to do that He would have had to take the love I had for my babies away, and that wasn't possible. Instead, He wrapped His arms around me and He stayed with me while I was grieving for my babies. The Atonement of Christ offers us more than just forgiveness of sins. While you may feel alone during this time of grieving, remember that He knows and understands all the pain, the fear, the anger, the guilt, and the sadness. Doctrine and Covenants 88:6 reminds us that "He that ascended up on high, as also he descended below all things, in that he comprehended all things, that he might be in all and through all things, the light of truth." He who has descended below all things can offer you the comfort that you cannot find from anyone else on Earth. He did not leave me comfortless, and He has promised that those who mourn shall be blessed, for they, too, shall be comforted.

Selected Bibliography

Kübler-Ross, Elisabeth. *On Death and Dying.* New York: Scribner Publishing, 1969.

Kübler-Ross, Elisabeth and David Kessler. *On Grief and Grieving.* New York: Scribner Publishing, 2005.

Wittwer, Sherri Devashrayee. *Gone Too Soon: The Life and Loss of Infants and Unborn Children.* American Fork, Utah: Covenant Communications, 1994.

About The Author

CAMILLE WHITING GRADUATED FROM BRIGHAM Young University with a bachelor of science degree in social work. She is currently busy raising eight children. Camille and her husband James's love of children and desire to involve their own children in serving others led them to become foster parents. It was through foster care that they were able to adopt twin sons. They experienced the devastating loss of their son Ammon and, several years later, of their daughter Kija. Over the years Camille has reached out to others in similar situations in the hope that she could provide an understanding ear. Camille's greatest happiness and fulfillment come through the joy of motherhood. Her other interests include writing, organizing, running, and music.